Beyond Discipline

Beyond Discipline

Parenting that Lasts a Lifetime

Edward R. Christophersen, Ph.D.

Overland Press, Inc.
9853 Rosewood
Shawnee Mission, KS 66207-3229

Cover Design: Lighthaus Design Group, Inc.
Cover Photography: Joe Rainaldi
Text Illustrations: Danny Whitehead

ISBN 0-930851-06-4

Printed in The United States of America
SECOND EDITION, 1998

Table of Contents

Preface . . . . *vii*

Acknowledgments . . . . *xi*

Introduction 1

The Importance of Touch 4

Communicating with Your Child 19

Self-Quieting Skills 28

Independent Play 56

Redirecting Your Child 75

Cognitive Development 81

Self-Esteem 87

Parent Coping Skills 93

Concluding Remarks 107

Suggested Additional Readings 109

Summary Handouts 111

    Infant Massage 113

    Preventing Excessive Crying with your Infant 115

    Testing your Infant's Self-Quieting Skills 117

    Teaching Self-Quieting Skills to Toddlers 119

    Teaching Independent Play Skills—Infants 121

    Teaching Independent Play Skills—Toddler 123

    Separation Anxiety 125

    Day Correction of Bedtime Problems 127

    Promoting Good Sleep Habits in Children 129

    Time-In 131

    Discipline for Toddlers 133

    Using Time-Out for Behavior Problems 135

    Redirecting Your Child's Activities 139

    Communicating with your Child 141

About The Author 143

Preface

There has been so much written about child rearing — parents write for other parents, professionals write for other professionals, and professionals write for parents — that we may have lost sight of why all of this writing has taken place and why people read what has been written. Most parents don't raise their children to please professionals or even to please other parents. Most raise their children in the hope that the children will end up being able to survive (in the emotional and social sense) as adults. What the child ends up doing, in terms of his or her profession, rarely seems to be part of this equation. Parents just want their children to end up doing something that they enjoy and, hopefully, something that they are good at. Parents want their children to become good, productive citizens. If their children also end up with a comfortable economic existence, that's fine. But the "bottom line" for parents seems to be that they want their children to end up with joy and competence. With this in mind, you would think that at least the professional writers would have identified, long ago, what skills children need to *survive* as adults and then proceed to provide detailed discussions on how to teach children these survival skills. Such has not been the case. If you ask the average parent why they are teaching, or trying to teach their children a particular skill, rarely does the answer include something dealing with long-term survival skills. Rather, the answer typically suggests a skill or an emotional state that the parent feels their child needs this day, this week, or this year.

One variable that totally confounds any parent's decision about what is best for his or her child is the parent's emotion. So many times parents will make a decision about their child based upon their own discomfort — they give in to a crying child, not because it's best for the child or even best for the adult, but because it relieves the parents' distress. In such cases, there is rarely a "big picture." The parents don't have anything approaching a long-term plan. When parents "let a child cry it out," usually neither the parent nor the child knows how they got into that situation in the first place and neither knows how to get out of it. Again, it's a today or this-week solution, not a solution that has the long-term best interest of the child in mind. Interestingly, the long-term best interest of the child is almost always in the best interest of the parent. In the long term, it is almost always easier on both the parent and on the child.

But think about this for a moment. Even a parent with incredibly good common sense or incredibly good intuition is not in a position to look at the long-term survival of their children because doing so requires a perspective that is unlike any perspective that the parent has ever had before. Parents know that a child who becomes a physician or an attorney is going to be better off financially, than one who is unemployed. Or do they? I'm convinced that such choices are just another symptom of the fact that parents really don't even know how to gauge what is in the child's best interest over the long term. On the one hand, many parents want their children to get an education and to get into a position in life that will provide them with the financial security that will allow them to do what they want to do. Yet, if you look at the statistics on both impaired physicians and impaired attorneys, they are substantially higher than in either the general population or in professionals in general.

This book is written from the perspective of a clinical psychologist who has worked in a pediatric setting, with normal families and normal children, for almost 20 years, and who provided clinical services, either personally or through clinical staff members under his supervision, for over 4,000 families. Many of these families have stayed in touch over the years, providing me with a perspective on the long-term survival that few professionals will ever have the privilege to enjoy. And the interesting part is that many of the children who, at least at the time, gave their parents grave concern, have turned out to be good, decent, successful adults, many of whom are now raising their own children and doing a very good job. And some of the children who appeared to be doing very well during their early years have never really been able to get their lives together and are still floundering as adults. There are directly discernable reasons why some children turn out just fine and some do not, and this book will discuss these reasons at some length, and will give many examples, all from real children and real families.

If successful, this book will probably stimulate a number of other books that pretend to address the same topic — long-term survival, or with similar words that convey the same basic tenet. Just remember, if the author of these books don't have the perspective that can only be derived from long-term contact with many normal children from early childhood until early adulthood, they are probably having a good time speculating at how to encourage children to become good people, but they have never researched the topic (that is, intentionally made suggestions and/or recommendations, with long-term survival as the primary goal). Most would be retrospective looking back, through opaque, rose-colored glasses, at children chosen because they were happy and successful.

Traditionally, all mental health services have been pathology based. Until recently, virtually all of the clinical training facilities for mental health professionals, even the ones considered to be the very best, have dealt with a disturbed population. They've dealt with individuals and their familes who sought services because they were distressed, unhappy, miserable, or downright disturbed.

For years, pediatricians and family practitioners have been the only professionals who routinely saw children over a long span of time. Unfortunately, owing to the time constraints of their practices, they never have had the time to spend with their young patients. One often-quoted study found that the average pediatrician spends less than two minutes during a typical well-child office visit talking with parents about their child and teaching them how to handle the wide variety of questions and concerns that parents of young children have. On the other hand, psychologists, psychiatrists, and social workers have almost all been trained in mental health settings where the prerequisite for being provided with services is that the individual child is "having problems." Daycare workers and professionals interested in early education of children have had a wonderful opportunity to deal with children intensely for a year or two but then the child outgrows their facility or their program and the child moves on, or, as they say in the research literature, the child is "lost to follow up."

Only recently have training programs like ours been educating young professionals to deal with normal families. Our staff spent enough time with each family that we can actually gain a perspective on what specific survival skills are really necessary and which look good at the time but wash out in the long run. The trainees that we have produced have usually had extensive experience with young, normal families. The fact that my practice has remained in the same community since its inception has made maintaining contact with these families a relatively easy task.

Just what skills qualify as survival skills? Which ones seem to be so important and what can be done to promote the development of these skills in children? What activities or interactions between parents and their children promote these skills and how can they be actively encouraged?

The chapters that follow will answer these questions and a whole lot more.

Acknowledgments

Over the past 20 years, there has been a remarkable consistency to the people who I could count upon for support. My immediate family has been the most supportive. My wife, Miki; my son, Hunter; and my daughter, Cathy; have been and continue to be an inspiration. My editor and dear friend, Barbara Cochrane, has read, edited, and improved much of what I have written. My students, interns, and fellows, who, by tactfully challenging most of what I have to say have forced me to challenge my own thinking, often effected changes that may not have taken place without their insightful and sometimes inciting remarks. The thousands of families that I have seen in my clinical practice over the past 20 years have been my motivation. My desire to help them, and their need for that help, has produced what you will read in the forthcoming pages.

Introduction

There are certain important skills that children need regardless of whether they come from single-parent families, adoptive families, step families, or foster families. They need these skills whether one, both, or neither parent works. They need these skills as children, as adolescents, and as adults.

Parents cannot punish their children if they don't have these skills, nor will repeated punishment produce or teach them. The age-old argument of whether to spank children simply does not apply here. All the spankings in the world won't teach these skills. Nor will taking away privileges, reasoning, or bribing. When present in children, these skills reduce the stress on the parents **and** help children to deal with their own stress. Without these skills, children are often subjected to unnecessary stress as are their parents.

These skills are important for children at play, for children in school, for teenagers in school and at work, and for adults at work and in their social lives.

These aren't newly discovered skills. Research has been conducted on them for many years (by such prestigious researchers as Dr. T. Berry Brazelton, Dr. Ashley Montegue and Dr. Tiffany Fields) — research that has verified, virtually every time they've been studied, how important these skills are in the development of a confident, secure, and productive adult. The only thing that hasn't been done before, with these skills, is to show how they relate to one another, how important they are to a child's academic and personal development, and how important they are to the development of a child's self-esteem.

These skills — **self-quieting, independent play, redirecting,** and **communication** — need to be *encouraged* rather than *tauqht*. These skills often exist in children who have bonded well with their parents, but this isn't necessarily so. The mere physical proximity of parent to child does not automatically produce an attachment between parent and child. However, children with good skills for self-quieting, independent play, redirecting, and communication almost always have a good relationship with their parents. This is probably because the skills that parents need in order to encourage these skills in their children are not necessarily common sense — they are learned.

Another unique quality of these skills is that encouraging them in children, regardless of the child's age, is often difficult for parents to do. Parents must endure uncomfortable feelings — feelings that they would prefer not to have — and feelings that, left unchecked, would otherwise motivate parents to pass on encouraging children to develop these important skills.

There are no known correlations between the presence of these skills and the wealth or education of a family. They do seem to correlate well with whether or not the parents have the skills themselves. When parents don't have these skills, they are not likely to attempt to encourage them in their children — it's just too uncomfortable to do so.

These skills are also a little unusual in that some children are born with them (as has been shown by the work with newborns done by Dr. Brazelton) and some children aren't. For years we knew about these skills, but we kind of assumed that children either had them or they didn't. Now we know better — now we know that these skills can be encouraged in children of all ages.

These skills are often seen in children who do not have behavior problems, in those children who go to bed without a hassle every night, who get toilet trained in a reasonable length of time, and who not only get decent grades in school, but who also do well in the work force.

At times, I've referred to these skills as *survival skills*, for without them, the road that children must pass is immeasurably harder for them and the people around them. Let's see what these skills are, how we can encourage them, and how much weight they carry in the development of adult personalities.

Let's see how we can help our little people develop into great adults — into adults who can handle the stress of raising children, or working, or both — adults who are equipped to deal with the lifestyles that they are likely to encounter.

1

The Importance of Touch

There is no activity that parents engage in with their children that is more important than physical contact. The demand characteristics of newborns and infants are such that a great deal of physical contact is necessary, if nothing else, for routine maintenance. Parents of infants change 70 to 100 diapers each week, bathe their baby daily, and dress and undress their baby at least several times each day, and we're not even counting the times the infant is picked up to comfort, to move around, or to carry! In some respects it is unfortunate that older children do not have the same demand characteristics as infants. Parents of a school-age child or adolescent do not *have* to have physical contact with them. Parents can go for long periods of time without much in the way of physical contact with their older child. The perfunctory hug here and kiss there just isn't enough. Nor is the obligatory praise for a job well done. Children of all ages simply cannot and do not live well without a lot of physical contact from their caregivers.

There is a condition in some children, sometimes referred to as *psychosocial dwarfism* where children do not eat much and they do not gain weight. Usually when these children are hospitalized for tests they gain weight and then, when they are discharged to their homes their appetite diminishes and they cease gaining weight. Although most children never reach this severe a point, there are still children who are not getting as much physical contact as they need. Just as children need food and water every day, they also need physical contact every day.

For parents or other caregivers who did not have much physical contact from their parents, this kind of physical contact is often hard to do because it doesn't come naturally and it doesn't feel natural. Also, children who aren't accustomed to a lot of physical contact may be distracted by it until they become more comfortable with it.

Infants

Touch has an effect that is far greater than simple caregiving. Touch has a calming effect. Many parents know that touch has this calming effect because they get into the habit of picking up their infant every time that the infant cries. Parents usually aren't aware that they are able to reduce or prevent that crying by providing physical contact *prior* to the crying. So, if your baby is on the floor, on a blanket, just looking around or sucking on her hand, brief physical contact with her has the same calming effect that it does when she's crying. But you don't have to wait for the crying to occur!

If you are currently picking your baby up, in response to her crying, about 15 times each day (which is very normal), try picking her up 20 to 25 times each day *before* she begins crying. Following this strategy reduces her crying because her need for physical contact is already being met without crying. But, in addition to picking your baby up, you should be providing her with brief, nonverbal, physical contact from 50 to 100 times each day — when she isn't fussing or demanding attention. So, if your baby is on the floor playing quietly or just looking around, make yourself get into the habit of giving her brief physical contact when she doesn't "need" it. This touching should only last 2 or 3 seconds. Resist the temptation to talk to her during these brief physical touches. The reason you should resist talking is that talking has a real tendency to disrupt whatever your baby may be doing. You will probably also find that it is easier to have physical contact with your baby when you are tired or when you are angry with someone else, than it is to verbally praise her. With brief physical touches, your own feelings that you have at the time don't get in the way as much as they do with verbal praise.

Some professionals actually recommend that you have set times during the day when you massage your baby. They usually say that you should massage her three times each day. This massage begins with placing your baby on her back, with her head facing towards you. Massage her head, across the sides, and then around the muscles on her face. Move down to her torso and massage her chest, then her arms, and her legs. Turn her over and do the same thing, starting with the back of her head and her neck and work down her torso, arms, legs, and feet. These three massage periods should only last about five minutes. As you become more comfortable and sure with yourself and with the infant massage, you will probably see that your baby enjoys these times. (See "Kisses from Heaven" for more information on infant massage.)

There was a study conducted in Florida, by Dr. Tiffany Fields and her colleagues, with premature babies in a hospital intensive-care unit. Half of the babies received routine intensive care and half of them received routine intensive care plus several infant massages each day. The babies who received the infant massage gained weight faster and were discharged to their homes sooner.

One caution with physical contact with infants — while it is alright to have times when you carry your baby around with you, the baby needs some balance. There must be times when your baby is away from you and learning to be calm on her own.

Parents who are constantly carrying their babies are teaching them that the way to be calm is to be carried and babies learn this lesson well. **It's important that there be some balance between time when the parent is carrying the baby and time when the baby is content to be alone.** Many babies don't come with self-quieting skills so they must be taught them. It's a well-established fact that teenage mothers and other mothers who are under an abnormal amount of stress, tend to carry their babies more than mothers who don't have a lot of stress or who handle their stress better. Apparently the reason that they carry their babies so much is so that they don't have to put up with as much of the baby's crying. As long as they are carrying their babies everywhere that they go, the babies do cry less, but, in the long run, these babies will probably end up crying more because they have never learned the skills for entertaining themselves and they have no opportunity to learn self-quieting skills. So, even though it seems easier for parents to carry their baby much of the time, in the long run, they are going to end up with a baby who cries more than the average baby and with a baby who lacks the skills necessary to self-quiet.

If you like to use a cloth carrier to make carrying your baby around easier on your arms and your back, be aware that a baby can be seriously injured if you are carrying her in a cloth carrier and you trip and fall. **I recommend that you not use cloth carriers outside your home and that you not use them on stairways within your home.** If you should fall down on a hard surface, while carrying your baby in a cloth carrier, you will probably hurt your baby with your own weight as you come into contact with the floor or the ground. There isn't time to protect yourself once the fall starts so it's better to avoid these situations in the first place. I know that there are some strong advocates of these clothcarriers, but I don't know any of these advocates who caution parents about the possibility of falls with your baby in one. All it takes is one fall to hurt a baby seriously — don't take the chance.

Toddlers

Although toddlers can be very active, a lot of physical contact, when the toddler is already calm, can lead to much greater periods of calm and much less need for discipline. If a toddler is looking through a book, or playing with his toys, many brief, nonverbal, physical contacts will prolong the length of time that he is playing and induce calmer play activities. An important distinction here is that the physical contact should be calming, not stimulating or distracting. Some parents get into the habit of playing rough with their toddler, teasing him or tickling him. This kind of contact is likely to result in the toddler become *more* active. Generally, we recommend that any roughhousing with a child should be done outside rather than inside your home. The reason for recommending that all roughhousing be done outside is that your child will begin to associate roughhousing with being outside and be less likely to insist on roughhousing inside. Children can also make the distinction between inside and outside much better than they can between a time when it's alright to roughhouse inside and a time when it's not alright to roughhouse inside.

Aggressive play with toddlers should be eliminated or discouraged. If you have relatives who like to play aggressively with your child, try to discourage them from doing so. If there are neighborhood children who are aggressive, just gradually encourage your toddler to play with other less aggressive children, even if doing so means that you have to drive them to someone else's house, instead of letting them walk next door to play with an aggressive child. If your child tends to be aggressive, limit his television viewing to shows that are not. Although I have never believed that an aggressive television program will make an otherwise nicely behaved child into an aggressive child, I do believe that an aggressive child can be unnecessarily stimulated by watching an aggressive television program.

One sign that you are having enough physical contact with your child is that he begins to behave more affectionately towards you. If you watch television while gently stroking his head and his back, you may be surprised to find that he will gently stroke your head or back in return.

When my son was about three years old, I used to watch television while lying on the floor with my head on a pillow (I think that this was about the time that I needed glasses but hadn't gotten them yet so I needed to be close to the TV set). When I was watching the TV, I would state aloud, "there's room on the floor for one little boy." Inevitably, my son would come over to me and lie down on the floor with his head sharing the pillow. One evening I was watching TV and hadn't said anything to him. From several feet away I heard him say, "Is there room on the floor for one little boy?"

These gentle times, when parent and child have close physical contact, even without any words being exchanged, combine together to form very pleasant memories and good emotional bonding. These times, however, are to be selected by the parent for their calming qualities, and, more than anything else, the physical contact needs to be intermittent and *unnecessary*. I say *unnecessary* to distinguish this contact from the contact some parents have with their children that is required or *necessary*. An example of *necessary* contact would be the parent who helps a child to go to sleep by lying down with the child. Instead of teaching the child to remain calm, the parent is doing the calming for the child. This is a mistake that will be paid for later in the sense that most of the time these parents are teaching their child to go to sleep with adult assistance and the child becomes dependent on this assistance or they can't get to sleep by themselves.

School Age

As children get older, many of them do not want to have the really close physical contact that they enjoyed so much when they were younger, but most, if not all, children still need the brief physical contact from their parents. School-age children should be able to entertain themselves much better and, consequently, should be doing many more things on their own.

Many brief, nonverbal, physical contacts are all that is necessary. If your seven- or eight-year-old is watching TV, reading a book, coloring, or playing a game, you can approach her, gently pat her, and remove yourself, without ever seeing any recognition from her that she knew you were there. That's perfect! It means that you are having enough physical contact with her. You can gently stroke her hair while she is watching TV without ever saying a word. You will probably notice that she will come over to the sofa where you are sitting and just place herself in a position where it is easy for you to stroke her hair without either of you saying one word.

If your child is involved in a sport, such as soccer, or taking dancing lessons, you can merely stand behind her, while she is waiting for her turn, and gently rub the back of her neck or shoulders. Other parents and children may never even notice what you are doing. This type of contact simply says, "I care about you" without making any demands on her for a certain level of performance or competition. The physical contact should be there when her team is winning and when her team is losing. The physical contact should be independent of any accomplishment on the child's part. A big hug for a goal scored or a job well done is fine, but it is no substitute for the gentle type of physical contact that your daughter gets just for being there and being your daughter. You may find that this kind of gentle contact makes losing a game, or coming in second, much easier on your child because you have already given her the message that you care, independent of performance.

Adolescent

If your child has been raised with a lot of physical contact, then it's easy to keep it up into adolescence. Maybe there will be fewer big hugs and kisses, but the gentle physical contact can be continued on into adulthood. The physical contact may change into the form of back rubs, neck rubs, or, in the case of my son, having his back scratched.

While these forms of physical contact are different from the forms used with young children, they accomplish the same thing — physical contact between the parent and the child. It's interesting to note the number of times that you hear married couples say that there they don't have enough physical contact in their relationship — not sexual contact, but gentle, physical contact. Adolescents who are studying for a test, or working on a project of their own choosing or for an organization, still need brief, nonverbal, physical contact. These are situations where speaking to these adolescents may disturb their concentration on what they are doing, but gentle physical contact is well received. This brings us to the topic of comforting your children.

Calming Children with Physical Contact

There is a real tendency, particularly with young children, to not only want to comfort the child when things don't go his way but also to fix whatever it was that upset him. As he gets older, it becomes increasingly more difficult to fix things. I think that it is far better to calm the child and let him fix whatever it is that upset him. As he gets older, he will begin to expect your calming influence without your fix. While young children usually get upset by things that parents can correct, the older the child gets, the harder it is for his parents to fix the things that upset him. For example, with toddlers or young preschoolers, a parent can phone other parents if something mean has happened to their child, and, within reason, the other parents will usually be responsive to such a phone call. With a teenager, they'd probably be embarrassed to the point of tears if they knew that you had phoned another teenager's parents in an attempt to correct an upsetting situation.

If you start out with your toddler by comforting him and leaving it up to him to fix the situation that upset him, you will be helping him to 1) learn to calm himself, and 2) learn how to correct situations that are upsetting to him. While the necessity for these two sets of skills isn't obvious with young children, it gets more obvious with each passing year.

Physical Comfort with Adults

I've observed many times, with adults, that when it was difficult to come up with the "right" words, physical contact is all that was necessary in order to offer emotional support. At my Uncle Johnny's funeral, when I was about 15 years old, I was very sad about losing my favorite uncle until I noticed that my Aunt Mary was very, very shaky. After watching her for a couple of minutes, as she stood by the graveside in preparation for the graveside services, she looked like she was going to fall down. For reasons that I really can't explain, I immediately went to her (we had never been really close, but we had always liked each other) and stood next to her, with my arm around her waist supporting her. As she leaned towards me for support, I just helped to hold her up without ever saying a word. She seemed to immediately be stronger and I felt much less traumatized by the whole funeral ceremony. I noticed 30 years later, when my father died, that the people who offered the most comfort to me were the people who didn't say anything but who held my hand or who put their arm around me. In fact, the people who did say something were often perceived by me as saying the "wrong" thing. I didn't want to hear that he wasn't suffering anymore or that he was "better off now." Since there wasn't anything anyone could say to make me feel better, it seems that the best thing that they could do was to not say anything at all.

The Parent Who Doesn't Feel Comfortable with Physical Contact

Many parents were raised in homes where there just wasn't much physical contact with their parents. After the days of their parents bathing them and dressing them, the physical contact just seemed to be a thing of the past. These parents can, by almost forcing themselves, learn to be more physically affectionate with their children. If they force themselves early enough, while their children are still young enough to readily accept the physical contact, the children can help to foster the physical contact by the way they respond to it. The parents will be rewarded for their efforts at physical contact by calmer, more affectionate children.

It's not unusual for children who get a lot of physical contact from their parents to reciprocate. While the parent is watching television or is engaged in a conversation with another adult, children will often approach the parent just long enough to give a gentle pat and then go back to what they were doing.

Obnoxious Children

One very pleasant benefit of being calm and affectionate with your children, from infancy onward, is that your children will come to have an enormous appreciation for other people who are calm, affectionate, and caring, and, further, they will come to feel uneasy around children who are obnoxious or hateful. Although your child probably will not be able to explain verbally what it is they dislike about a new child that they meet, it's common for children who get accustomed to a warm and caring environment to feel a sense of discomfort when they are around obnoxious children. With both of my children they have, at times, started relationships with new children at their schools who were troubled — who came from homes where there was a lot of yelling and screaming and, I presume, more physical punishment than was probably good for the child. In every case, I can't remember either of our children continuing their relationships with the new child for more than one or two weeks. When asked why they weren't playing with a particular child anymore, they usually just said that they didn't enjoy playing with him, or that they didn't know why. They would simply prefer to stay at home without a playmate or play with some other child. While I understand that this may not be the best thing for the obnoxious child, my children are children, not therapists, and their job is to be children, not to try to save the neighborhood rejects.

Bathing and Sleeping with your Children

Although I know that many parents who bath and/or sleep with their child will say that they are doing it for the child, in my experience they are doing it because it makes the parents feel better, because it results in the child fussing less, at least initially. If your child can sleep by himself every night, go to sleep with little fussing and sleep through the night, then I don't see anything wrong with occasionally letting him sleep with you. The interesting observation here, though, is that children who go to sleep easily alone and sleep through the night, usually associate sleeping with their own bed and, when tired or not feeling well, they will usually say that they want to go to bed, that they don't feel well or they are tired. Again, it's the parent who needs the comfort, and they will get this comfort even if it's at the child's expense. Isn't it sad that some parents value their own day-to-day comfort more than what they may be teaching their children? This is what we refer to as "short-term gain for long-term pain."

The Overactive Child

There are some homes that virtually always have at least one television set going, phone calls almost back-to-back, and, in general, a noise and activity level that would make it difficult for anyone to concentrate on anything.

Children who grow up in such a home have a good likelihood of appearing to be overactive. This is not to be confused with children who have Attention Deficit Disorder which is a verifiable diagnosis for children who are impulsive, easily distracted, and unable to complete one task before starting another. Overactive children are children who have been exposed to so much stimulation that they become habitually more active than most of the other children their age. Overactive children don't need a bunch of testing and they don't need to be medicated. What they need, when they are growing up, is a calm, sane environment in which to live —one where there is actually time spent with no television set on, no radio on, and no one talking. While this may sound almost impossible, it can actually be quite enjoyable. It's also interesting to note that children from homes that encourage overactivity also almost completely lack the kind of gentle, calm, physical contact that I've been discussing throughout this book. If you have an overactive home, here are some guidelines to consider:

Quiet Time

A period of time should be set aside each evening during which no phone calls are taken or placed, no television set or radio is turned on, and no visitors or guests. If you aren't used to having quiet time, it may be a good idea to start slowly so that the withdrawal pains aren't too severe.

Even if you begin with 15 minutes of quiet each evening, that's an improvement over no quiet time. During quiet time, everyone in the house is expected to engage in a quiet activity — quiet both in terms of the noise that they are making and quiet in terms of the amount of movement that they are making. Thus, quiet activities might include reading, paying the bills, balancing the checkbook, coloring, or putting together a puzzle alone. Activities such as games, videogames, reading aloud to your children, and verbal discussions are discouraged. Even though overactive children have a hard time, initially, tolerating the lack of stimulation, they can usually adjust to it as least as quickly as their parents do.

Over time, children learn to appreciate how much they can get done with some peace and quiet. It doesn't matter whether they are just organizing their rooms, sorting through their schools papers, or actually doing homework. It's the daily quiet time that encourages them to get things done.

Many parents will say that their children never read or do things quietly at home, but when you ask them, they will tell you that there really isn't any quiet time in their homes. I can't concentrate on anything when there is a lot going on and I don't think that children are much different.

If your children learn, from experience, that you are going to enforce and honor, yourself, quiet time on school nights, over time they will be better able to use that time. Sure, they may flounder for a couple of weeks while they learn to use their new found time, but eventually they will probably learn to use their time better. The difficulty with enforcing and honoring quiet time is that the parents have to be a part of it. If you tell your children that they must be quiet for the next hour and then you get on the phone or go into the back bedroom to watch a football game or a sitcom, you're giving your children a mixed message. It's difficult to learn to manage your own time effectively, but this is a skill that children can use all of their lives. Some children have about 10 to 12 hours of quiet time each week. Most of the time they may use this time for doing homework or reading. However, some of this time can be used to clean up their rooms. Typically, the children who must be forced into cleaning up their rooms do the poorest job of cleaning, mainly because they don't have any plan or format in mind — all they are doing is "cleaning up" in order to get you off of their case. The child who can comfortably spend hours in their room alone, including doing their homework, enjoying a hobby, or cleaning and straightening, is much more likely to have a clean room and to know where things are than a child who is rarely using their room for anything constructive. When children are forced or coerced to clean their rooms they will usually just get everything out of sight. They aren't logically putting anything away, where they can easily find it later. Rather, they're just trying to satisfy you by making their room "look" neat. Whether or not they can find anything is immaterial. All they are trying to do is "get you off of their back." However, don't be misled by neatness. If your child has what looks like a messy room, but they get a lot done in their room and they can always find what they need — they may very likely have their priorities better than a child with a neat room who otherwise doesn't get anything done in their room.

One other important feature of quiet time is that the parents have to provide their children with lots of gentle, nonverbal, physical contact during quiet time. The physical contact encourages the children to continue with the quiet time until such time as the children begin to derive their own enjoyment out of it. Once children learn to enjoy activities such as reading, they can often continue to enjoy it for the rest of their lives. An investment of 15 to 30 minutes per evening for the six months to a year that it takes to get a child acclimated to quiet time is a small price to pay for a lifetime return.

If you set aside specific times each evening during the week when the house will be quiet, when no TVs or radios are on, and no phone calls are placed or accepted, you will probably find that your house becomes more pleasant. The point here, and a point that I've tried to make throughout this book, is that children shouldn't clean up their rooms because they will get disciplined if they don't and they shouldn't read a book because they will get disciplined if they don't. But, they also shouldn't be expected to clean their room because they have an inner need to have a clean room. Room cleaning should come as a natural activity, an activity that is *necessary* for them to be able to find their things, an activity that fills a function or a need for your child. Such children usually not only have neater rooms than other children, but their parents will typically report that they don't have any trouble getting their children to "keep their rooms neat." This is because the clean room serves a function for the child. The clean room is merely a means to another end. Trying to teach a child that a neat room, in and of itself, is a highly desirable goal in life is a bit silly and unrealistic.

Modelling

Parents who never do anything useful in the presence of their children aren't doing either themselves or their children any favors. I've heard many parents say that they don't do anything useful when their children are awake because they can't concentrate. It's almost as though they would have me believing that the presence of children makes quiet time prohibitive. In fact, if the parents begin modelling good use of quiet time from infancy on, the children will adjust to it naturally and come to appreciate it for what it is — peace and quiet. While I have to admit that initially parents won't get much done during this quiet time, once the children learn to use this time, everyone in the house will get some benefit from it. It's also easier to get children to bed if their bedtime was preceded by quiet time. You don't have to wait for the children to unwind when they have just gone through 30 minutes of quiet time.

The Strong-Willed Child

There's nothing wrong with a determined, strong-willed child, as long as she has some direction to her life. Most of the successful managers in the Fortune 500 companies are strong-willed individuals who can concentrate for long periods of time, who know what they want, and who know how to block out distractions. A strong-willed child who has excellent self-quieting skills, plays well independently, and is well disciplined is an asset to almost any family and later to schools and to corporations. Typically, however, when we talk about a strong-willed child, we are talking about a strong-willed child who is not well disciplined, who doesn't self-quiet very well, and who doesn't have much in the way of independent play skills. This can also be referred to as a tyrant. The strong-willed child can be raised exactly the same way, with the same priorities that you would have with a child of average determination. The major difference is that the child rearing will be more difficult for the child's parents, and the pay back, in terms of what the child is able to accomplish on her own, later in life, is greater.

2

Communicating with Your Child

Most parents incorrectly assume that communicating with their children involves asking questions or explaining things. Communication does include two-way conversations, but the one-way conversations, where we listen to a child and try to understand what they are saying and feeling are infinitely more important. We seem to have a difficult time remembering that the most satisfying communication, in our own lives, is when a person whom we consider important will listen to us and try to understand what we are saying. While there are important times for verbal dialogues, there are more times when listening is important.

Infants

The most important communication with an infant is the physical contact that we have with them. Holding them, cuddling with them, picking them up when they are distressed, feeding them when they are hungry, and putting them to bed when they are tired are all part of this communication process. Certainly the demand characteristics of infants are such that we have to pick them up a lot, but we also need to concentrate on providing them with **brief, non-verbal, physical contact when they don't need it.** When an infant is lying on the floor, sucking on her hand or playing with her fingers, you can frequently and gently touch her on the back, or rough up her hair. While this may interrupt her momentarily at first, she will quickly get to the point where she doesn't even seem to notice the contact. Don't think for one moment that she doesn't like it. What you should notice, over a period of time, is that she will play for increasingly longer periods of time on her own.

A variation of this theme is brief verbal contact with infants. If you are taking a bath, fixing your hair, making dinner, or working on your taxes or balancing your checkbook, you can frequently, but briefly, talk to your infant, for just a moment, then return to what you were doing. While the talking is clearly no substitute for physical contact, it can complement the physical contact.

Toddlers

The activity level of toddlers is sometimes almost overwhelming. As they travel about their home, they cover practically every square foot several times a day. To just wait until they get into trouble and then discipline them for what they did has one real basic flaw to it — discipline never teaches a child **what to do**, it only teaches him **what not to do**. Even more unpleasant than waiting for him to get into trouble is constantly warning him about the things that you don't want him to do. Most adults hate to be constantly warned or nagged about their behavior. I remember the father of a seven-year-old who told me how furious he was that his son had fallen asleep the night before in the middle of a "good talk." The good talk, as you may have guessed, consisted of the father lecturing and the child supposedly listening to the lecture. The child didn't fall asleep until after the lecture had lasted more than one hour. Children don't have the ability to operationalize conversations with adults. Just because you have warned your child repeatedly about the same bad behavior doesn't mean that he is going to change the way that he is behaving. Rather, the constant warnings will communicate to your child that you are unhappy with him and that you don't care about him.

Some parents seem to think that if they "chew out" their children nicely, without raising their voices or using bad words, that the children will like the chewing more. Nobody I know likes to get chewed out, regardless of their age. It is much like the fad several years ago that involved parents telling their children how irritated they were when their children engaged in inappropriate behaviors. These discussions were supposed to change the child's behavior. I can't count the number of children to whom I talked during this fad who said that they wished that their parents would stop nagging them. It seemed as though there was no end to either the child's bad behavior or the parent's nagging. Just because the parent says unpleasant things in a nice way doesn't mean that the child is going to like the chewing out. Like you and like me, the children would rather not hear about it at all.

A good habit to try to get into is to choose one or two situations in which you don't talk — you just wait for your child to talk and then you respond, as unemotionally as possible, to what they have to say. If, for example, you choose trips around town in the car for your "quiet time," it means that you will not use this time to get any messages across or to interrogate your child about an activity that they just completed or are just about to start. Now, initially, this is hard for parents to do. Most of us are very accustomed to picking our children up at school or at day care and immediately asking them what they did. All I'm suggesting is that you keep quiet until your child has something to say, then respond to her, unemotionally. So, instead of asking your daughter what she did at the day care center, you would just pick her up and drive home without saying anything. This way, if she had anything that she wanted to talk about, she would have the opportunity to bring it up. Don't be surprised, the first couple of times, if she doesn't say a word. If she's tired from playing at preschool, she might not have anything to say. Fine. Just leave well enough alone and be quiet. You may have to have quiet trips home from day care several times in a row before she figures out that you aren't going to dominate the time with your questions. After several quiet trips, your child will probably begin to talk about something that is completely unrelated to day care or school.

When my son was a toddler, I used to drive him to preschool two mornings each week. Following my own advice, I would drive him there without talking unless he spoke first. Over the course of several months, we watched a construction crew build a four-story building. One morning, when the workmen were putting in some of the utilities, my son must have noticed a toilet fixture on the top floor because he asked me, "What happens to poop that falls that far?" I thought about his question for a minute and told him that I had to admit that I didn't know, but that that was an excellent question. The point is that we, as adults, would never have thought of such a question. There was no indication what he was thinking about until he asked his question. It wasn't until several years later that I was using his question to make a point with a group of parents, one of whom was a sanitation engineer, that I found out what does happen to poop that falls that far. Now, I have to admit, I often think about this question when I am in a tall building for a meeting or to stay overnight.

If you are asked a question and you don't have the slightest idea of what the answer is, you can help teach your child problem-solving skills by answering the question with another question. "I don't know what happens to it, what do you think?"

The ensuing dialogue may help you to come up with the correct answer or you may end up concluding that neither of you knows the answer to the question.

While it is not possible for parents to always know the answers to their children's questions, they can still encourage their children's questions by being receptive, listening, understanding, and remaining nonjudgmental. Simple physical contact can convey to a child that it is alright for him to ask questions and, more than that, you can teach behavior without ever opening your mouth.

If a toddler is playing with anything from dolls to tin cans, a lot of brief, nonverbal, physical contact will encourage him to play like that for increasingly longer periods of time. The more time he plays the more opportunity you have to provide him with physical contact and the less time he has to get himself into trouble. After several months of providing a lot of brief, nonverbal, physical contact, it's sometimes surprising how much time he will spend on the types of behaviors that you want him to do and how little discipline you will need with him.

School Age

As children become more and more verbal, parents tend to lecture more to them, under the mistaken impression that the children are now at an age where they will profit more from the lectures. Nothing could be further from the truth. As children get older, the opinions of their peers take on more and more importance and what their parents have to say gets relegated to second place. Although children, as they get older, are less likely to listen to their parents, they still, like everyone else, want to be listened to. As I have discussed with toddlers, it's a good idea to establish situations in which you dependably keep your mouth shut. If your school-age child knows that you don't talk much in the car, then he comes to depend on those car rides as a time when he can talk if he wants to. Although there is absolutely no way to predict when or what he will have to say, it is safe to predict that he will say more things, more often, that are important to him if you are quiet than if you are dominating the conversation. True, much of these conversations will be about things that you don't think are important, but if your child thinks that they are important isn't that what counts? Too many times parents want to pick what they think is important to talk about, regardless of what their children want to talk about, and then they wonder why their children don't enjoy talking to them.

The First Rule of Communication Is Listening

If you get into the habit of listening to your children, then you won't have to talk to them — they'll tell you what's on their minds without you ever having to ask.

The Second Rule of Listening Is Understanding

When a child talks, they may not say things the same way an adult would and, if taken literally, we may misinterpret what she is saying. For this reason, it's a good idea to restate in your own words what your child is saying to make sure that you understand that point that he or she was trying to make.

The Third Rule of Listening Is to Refrain from Judging your Child

Your daughter cannot tell you something that is very important to her (and that she is a little apprehensive talking about) if she knows that you are going to get angry with her for saying such a thing. For example, if your daughter asks you a question about a dirty poem that she saw at school and you immediately begin a sermon about how you will not have that kind of filth in your home, then your daughter never really got the chance to discuss dirty poems with you (why people write them and why people like them). Basically, you leave her no opportunity to discuss such a topic with you. If she's going to ask anyone about dirty poems, it will have to be someone outside of her home.

Adolescents

There is probably nothing more embarrassing to a teenager than to have their parents nagging or warning them in front of their friends. It's fine to tell a teenager that you want them home by a certain time or that you want them to call you if they decide to go someplace other than where they originally set out for. Again, it's the lectures and the warnings that take their toll more than any matter-of-fact statement to be sure to call home (or better yet, have your adolescent show you their quarter that they have in case they should need to call home).

I remember a very nice couple who called me about their 13-year-old daughter, whom I'd seen a few months earlier in my office. Their daughter was caught hand copying an obscene poem during one of her classes at school. Her teacher, who was somewhat appalled by the vulgarity of the poem, instructed the girl to give the poem to her parents when she got home from school. That evening the teacher called the parents and found out that the girl had never told her parents about the poem. The girl's father ordered her to give him the poem and to go up to her room for an hour, at the end of which she would have to tell her mother and father what every bad word in the poem meant. Then the parents called me.

After they got over the original rush of trying to convey to me exactly how disgusting the whole incident was to them, I asked them if they had taught their daughter all of the details about sex. They said they had, but they had never talked to her like this. We discussed their daughter's sex education in more detail, long enough to find out that sex education, to them, consisted of a description of the mechanics of reproduction including the physiology of the female reproductive system, menstruation, and personal hygiene. When I informed them that they had just started their "sex education" about 20 minutes ago and so far they weren't doing so well they both seemed very puzzled. They kept referring back to that dirty old poem. I reminded them that a number of 13-year-old girls in this city were already mothers, that many were pregnant, and that their daughter had a right to think about whatever she wants to think about and to talk to her friends about whatever she wants to talk about. In fact, their daughter's only mistake was that she allowed herself to get caught with the poem.

Parents need to be sensitive about their adolescent's sexuality. They may be able to raise a teenager who does not act out her sexuality but she still has a right to think about and talk about it with her friends. This situation at least had the appearance of a teenager who felt much more comfortable talking with her friends than with her parents. This may have been due to the fact that her parents couldn't separate their own feelings about sexuality from their feelings for their daughter. Fortunately, I was able to convince them to back off on their own needs to discipline their daughter and to recognize that she was actually handling her sexuality very well. They should be proud of how well their daughter was doing. Discipline, in this situation, wasn't really necessary. What was necessary was a more open line of communication between the daughter and her parents.

Many times parents become too concerned about what their teenagers are talking about. They don't give them enough credit for how they are behaving. A responsible teenager who is getting good grades in school, who has a well-behaved support group, and who has managed their sexuality well deserves the benefit of the doubt when an indiscretion is suspected — particularly when the indiscretion is verbal and not behavioral. The biggest risk for parents in a situation like this is that they may become too punitive and try to force any hint of sexuality out of their teenager. Parents need to be able to discuss sexuality with their son or daughter beyond the mechanics and hygiene of sex and address the feelings about sex that are often so difficult for a teenager to deal with. A teenage girl may be able to figure out how to deal with her menstruation from reading and from talking to her friends, but her parents are probably in the best position to help her deal with her feelings about sexuality.

3

Self-Quieting Skills

Everyone of us has had an untold number of occasions when we have had a less than desirable interaction with another adult, a time when we wanted to give them "a piece of our mind" and we didn't. On those occasions when we didn't, we used what are referred to as self-quieting or self-consoling skills. Some babies come with good self-quieting skills and most that don't come with them can be taught them. Most of us can immediately think of people that we know who have a great deal of patience. In some cases, we may even envy these people. We often say that they sure are lucky because they don't get mad. Yet, in actuality, it probably takes just as much effort for them to keep their mouth shut as it does for us. Maybe they have better skills, but it still takes effort to do it.

I'm reminded of the time that I was checking in at a TWA airline counter for a crowded flight to the East Coast. The agent at the ticket counter had asked whether I wanted "smoking" or "non-smoking" and I had responded, "nonsmoking." She informed me, apologetically, that she only had a seat in Row 28, which was direct-ly in front of the first row of smokers. When I responded that "that was fine," she said that I was one of the first people that day who hadn't yelled at her. After saying thanks, I told her that as I travel so much I try to be nice to people, partially because I'm almost certain to encounter them again. As she handed me the boarding pass for Row 28, she said that she would try to get me a better seat if she could. As I was waiting to hand my boarding pass to the person at the gate, after my section was called to board, she ap-proached me — I had a briefcase in one hand and carry-on luggage in the other — she took the boarding pass for Row 28 out of my suit coat pocket and slid in a replacement, telling me that she was successful at getting me a better seat. When I got to the boarding agent, I found out that she had given me a boarding pass for a first-class seat. I certainly didn't see her doing any favors for the people who had been giving her a hard time.

In those situations where each of us is less than thrilled at what's happening to us and where we'd do anything we could to change things, most of the time there simply isn't anything else that can be done. When we don't like what's happening and we are able to keep our mouths shut, we are using self-quieting skills. Even those of us who have had one of the old assertiveness training workshops, or something similar to that have to have self-quieting skills before we can exercise the assertiveness training skills.

In virtually all situations that we encounter that are unpleasant to us, the first and most important skill we must have is the ability to keep our mouths shut until we've had a minute to assess the situation and arrive at what would be the best solution for us. Self-quieting skills can almost always buy us a couple of minutes of time, precious time, before we let our response be known to other people. Most adults have at least two options. We can let another person really have it, or we can keep our cool and see how things develop. As long as we have both sets of skills, we can choose which set of skills we want to exercise. If, however, we don't have these self-quieting skills, then we have only one choice, and that's to let the other person have it. In the case of the frustration we may feel when we're working with an inanimate object, such as the plumbing in our home, we have the choice of yelling and swearing at the broken plumbing or keeping our temper while we analyze the situation for a workable solution.

One variation of this are adults who get furious but who don't say anything. Even though they aren't showing it, they don't have any self-quieting skills, but it isn't as obvious as it would be if they were ranting and raving. They may look like they are "handling the situation" but they are barely any better off than the individual who gets outwardly angry. In fact, these are the people who are technically called *hot reactors*.That is, they get very upset but they don't necessarily let it be known to other people.

Many of the people who you know have "problems with their temper" are just grown-ups who don't have any self-quieting skills; which means that we can reduce the problems that children will have later, with anger, if we will make sure that we teach them good self-quieting skills when they are still young. It does seem that the younger we start on teaching children self-quieting skills, the easier and quicker it is to do it.

Where Does It All Start?

During early infancy, it is possible to tell how well an individual infant does at self-quieting. Within the first few days of life, some newborns are able to calm themselves down within one or two minutes of the time that they get upset. There's a test, developed by Dr. T. Berry Brazelton and his colleagues, that is performed on infants before they are one month old, that assesses how well the infant self-quiets. With this test, an otherwise happy and content infant is startled or awakened to produce crying. Then the infant is observed for two full minutes to see if he is capable of calming himself down. If an infant can calm himself down, he has demonstrated very good self-quieting skills. If, after two minutes, the infant cannot self-quiet, then the adult who is administering the test begins to "help" the infant more and more with each step, giving the infant sufficient time with each step to self-quiet if he has the skills. If the infant cannot self-quiet alone, then the tester will stand with his face about one foot above the infant and speak to the infant in a normal voice tone for one minute.

If the infant still has not quieted down, then he will continue speaking to the infant and also hold the infant's hands firmly against the infant's chest. As the steps progress, the adult provides more and more assistance until such time that the infant can quiet down.

The main reason that I recommend testing self-quieting skills in a newborn is so that you can see if your baby "came with" these skills. That is, if your baby can self-quiet at two or three days of age, you certainly can't claim any credit for teaching him or her those skills. You were just fortunate to have a baby with good self-quieting skills at birth. By the same token, if you have a newborn who apparently has poor self-quieting skills, you shouldn't be blamed for it either. Babies are individuals and as such there are differences right from the start.

Those infants who can self-quiet, without any assistance from an adult, are said to have good self-quieting skills, while those infants who need a great deal of help are said to have poor self-quieting skills. Self-quieting, during infancy, serves some very important functions. It isn't always possible for someone to meet an infants' needs immediately, although most infants do give adults the impression that the needs *better* be met immediately.

When faced with an infant who has good self-quieting skills, most adults don't have much trouble providing for her basic needs. I'm reminded of a time when friends of ours stayed at our home to watch our daughter, Cathy, who was less than one year old at the time. When Cathy awakened in the morning, she played quietly in her crib, having learned some time earlier that we would soon come to her room to change her diaper and feed her. When the friends heard her, they just waited, in bed, to catch some extra sleep and to see if Cathy was really up for the morning. After some time passed, Cathy fell back to sleep as did our friends. Cathy awakened again a few hours later and, this time, when she started playing in her crib, they did get up to take care of her. In this same situation, an infant with poor self-quieting skills probably would have screamed her guts out until someone came in to take care of her.

Some parents seem to get so hyper over a crying infant that they never allow the infant to self-quiet. Whenever their baby cries, no matter what the reason, they instantly come to her rescue. These parents usually don't even realize that they are not doing their baby a favor by jumping to meet her needs as quickly as they do. Nor, in the long run, are they doing themselves any favor. As their baby gets older, and they still have to cater to her every need or he or she will cry, and the parents will start to get increasingly more frustrated with the baby. If you do have a baby who doesn't seem to be able to self-quiet, you have two basic choices. You can either spend their entire childhood trying to figure out how to satisfy them, without necessarily having much in the way of clues, or you can teach the child self-quieting skills and make the rest of their life and your life easier and more enjoyable. I am not, of course, saying that parents shouldn't meet their infant's needs, or that they should let their infant cry all of the time. There is a big difference between letting a baby cry all of the time, with no real plan in mind and letting a baby cry, under carefully controlled conditions so that you can teach them a very important skill — self-quieting. Most infants will cry occasionally for no reason at all, except perhaps that they are bored, and, if left alone for a couple of minutes, they will usually self-quiet.

Here are some strategies to consider in teaching self-quieting skills to an infant:

Put Babies to Bed Awake but Drowsy

Some parents feel so uncomfortable hearing their baby cry at bedtime that they do anything possible to avoid hearing the crying. Thus, if they put their baby to bed and the baby doesn't go to sleep immediately, they go back in to see "what's wrong." In doing so, they prevent the child from ever learning how to quiet down. However, because they are able to quiet the baby down, they usually feel a sense of pride from doing so. A second feeling, and one not so readily admitted, is a sense of relief in getting the baby to quiet down. It is this sense of relief, and the parent not wanting to have the uncomfortable feeling of having to listen to a baby who is learning how to quiet down, that usually motivates parents to refuse to let their baby learn to self-quiet. Unfortunately, this self-serving relief is frequently responsible for parents getting into the habit of rescuing their children and thus keeping them from learning important skills.

Self-Quieting at Bedtime

The baby who is consistently put to bed and left there, after all of their other needs are met, whether they go to sleep in one minute or 15 minutes, almost always learns to self-quiet at bedtime. The baby who thus learns how to self-quiet can usually generalize this learning to the daytime and to the many daytime situations where self-quieting is a beneficial skill to have.

My classic case of a child with no self-quieting skills at bedtime was an 11-month-old boy whose mother had been ignoring his crying in the middle of the night, with no success, for six weeks (we practically never recommend that parents ignore children who wake up in the middle of the night crying). When the entire story became clear to me, the pattern that had caused this problem was very clear. The mother had been breast feeding her baby until he was asleep for his morning nap, for his afternoon nap, and for the evening, practically since his birth. Thus, when the baby would awaken in the middle of the night, he understandably needed his mother's assistance in order to get back to sleep. It took at least one hour to convince the mother that what she was doing during the day (feeding the baby to sleep for both naps and for the night) was directly contributing to his not being able to go to sleep by himself. In this instance, we said that the child had been taught *adult sleep-transition skills*. That means that he had been taught to go to sleep only when he mother was holding him and nursing him. After convincing the mother to put her baby to bed awake and to let him fall off to sleep by himself, his problems with awakening in the middle of the night resolved within one week. After going to sleep four times each 24 hours (for each nap, for the night, and once during the night) for a week, the baby had experienced how to go to sleep by himself 28 times. He had learned *self-transition skills*.

A child with self-transition skills can easily go to sleep alone most of the time. With infants, self-transition skills often involve a physical object such as sucking a thumb or holding onto a blanket. Given the physical nature of these self-quieting skills, there are two additional considerations. First, parents must discipline themselves to not help the child to do this self-quieting. If your baby doesn't have a pacifier in her mouth and you go into her room to put it into her mouth, you have changed what could have been a self-transition skill to an adult transition skill. Sure, it might take a couple of nights for your baby to learn to reach around the crib to find the pacifier, but after learning that skill, it can be used for a long time Second, you need to have a number of objects in the area of the baby, such as a blanket and a couple of stuffed toys, that can potentially serve as transition objects. As children get older they become increasingly more likely to do their own self-quieting without needing any physical transition object.

When young children are developing their fine- and gross-motor skills, they commonly encounter situations where it would be easier if an adult did the task for them rather than having to do it themselves. I'm reminded of a one-year-old child whom I saw for developmental delays (he wasn't walking or talking yet) who was clearly ready for much more development, but whose parents couldn't tolerate the discomfort of allowing him to stumble a little bit before he walked. If he was sitting on the floor and wanted a red ball that was only a foot in front of him, he would cry out and one of his parents would pick up the ball and hand it to him. With another youngster, this time about 13 months old, his parents told me in the office that he couldn't crawl yet. After conducting the initial interview, we proceeded out to a play area that was covered with indoor-outdoor carpeting. We placed the baby on the floor and I did everything possible to engage the mother in conversation while one of my assistants tried to distract the father. Almost immediately the baby began to move towards the mother and me. I insisted that the mother back up with me, and, as we did, the baby moved a little more towards us. As we kept backing up, the baby kept moving towards us. His mother then verbalized that he had never crawled before. I said, "No. He's not crawling. He doesn't know how to crawl." The mother disagreed with me about three times until she realized that I was just teasing her — until she realized that her son could crawl if only she would "let him."

A number of years ago, we published a research study on the sleep habits of one-year-old children. We asked each set of parents to place an audio tape recorder in the baby's room and, whenever the parent said the "last" words to their baby (for example, "goodnight," or "I love you," or "see you in the morning," the parents were instructed to push the record button on a tape recorder. The recorders all had 30 minute tapes in them and then shut off automatically. When analyzing these tapes, we noticed two very interesting findings. One, when listening to the tapes of babies who went to sleep easily, without much fussing and crying, NONE of the tapes had any sounds of the parents coming back into the baby's room or talking to the baby. Two, when listening to the tapes of babies who had trouble getting to sleep, every one of them had sounds of the parents trying to "help" their baby get to sleep. Interesting too, was the fact that none of the "good" or "easy" babies went to sleep immediately. Everyone of them made some kind of sounds for at least a minute or two — maybe babbling or cooing, or sometimes fussing or crying. The point is, the "good" babies did show some fussy behaviors at bedtime but their parents left them alone to go to sleep and every one of them was able to do so. With the babies who had trouble getting to sleep, some of the parents were still coming into the baby's room a full 30 minutes after they had put the baby to bed.

Pick Up Cute Babies

Between birth and around 10 weeks of age, most babies wake up and cry immediately. But, after about 10 to 12 weeks of age, most babies will wake up and look around their room and make noises before they start crying. If the parent will get up immediately and go to the baby, during this time when they are making their cute little noises, then the baby will learn to make cute little noises upon awakening in the morning and from a nap.

If, on the other hand, the baby is left in the crib until he or she begins crying, they are being taught that they must cry if they want someone to come in and get up. The choice really is yours. Your baby doesn't care which way you do it — they just want attention when they get up from sleeping.

Many parents have read books that say that children never cry unless they have an "unmet need." Unfortunately, this kind of "advice" caters to the guilt that parents feel when they wait while their child has to stumble through a problem-solving task. Whether it's a baby crying at naptime or bedtime, or a toddler fussing because he doesn't want to eat new foods or nonpreferred foods, fussing is just part of being a child. The horror stories that come from meals with young children are worse than the ones about learning developmental skills. Experienced parents know that many children do not "like" it when new foods are included in their meals. I don't think that it's really that they don't like the new foods as much as it is that they aren't accustomed to them and they fuss when they first experience them.

Self-Quieting at Mealtimes

Many children fuss or cry when new foods are introduced at mealtimes. If a child has good self-quieting skills, then the parent can usually outlast the child until he has the opportunity to experience the new foods enough that he stops fussing about them. I don't mean that you should force a child to eat or that you should leave him sitting at the table until he eats a new food. I mean that, if you offer the new food on several different occasions, and your child fusses about the food until he self-quiets, he will eventually try the new food and may just decide that he likes it. The child with good self-quieting skills fusses for a little while and then resumes eating. **The self-quieting skills place a limit on the amount of fussing that the parent must endure before they have another opportunity to give the child the new food.** After a number of these kinds of meals, the parent begins to gain some confidence in their ability to get their child to do things that he doesn't want to do and the child begins to learn that the parent is not going to "help them" by taking away the nonpreferred food and going back to a preferred food. In doing so the child learns that there are many different flavors and textures to foods and inevitably the child learns to enjoy some of these new flavors and textures.

One of my favorite mealtime stories is about a toddler who would only eat meals if he was riding his tricycle in the kitchen. He would ride to one doorway where his mother was waiting with a spoonful of food. Then he would ride to the other doorway where his dad was waiting with another spoonful of food. The only way that he would eat (at least he had convinced his parents that this was the only way that he would eat) was by riding his tricycle. Other mealtime stories abound, but the basic theme is that parents would rather adapt their entire routine to suit a child than have the child fuss. It frequently ends up with the child actually in charge of the parents, using the parents' uncomfortable feelings about hearing their child cry to turn mealtimes and bedtimes into a fiasco. **Notice that I said that the parents' uncomfortable feelings are the primary motivator — not the child's feelings. These parents will usually talk a good tune, they say that they are doing what they are doing for the benefit of the child but that is indeed untrue. They are doing what they are doing at the expense of the child to make themselves feel better.**

Self-Quieting During Frustrating Times

Virtually every one of us has encountered a situation where we were very frustrated and we "lost it" (got angry, threw something, said something that wasn't nice). Many of us have been in situations where we were very frustrated and we managed to cope with it very well. If we have both sets of skills, then we have the option of choosing which skills we want to use. If we only know how to lose it, then we really don't have a choice.

With a toddler, a good example would be a toddler who is playing with some building blocks and the whole thing falls down unexpectedly. If the child just kicks the remaining construction parts down and walks away, that's an example of a frustrating event without adequate self-quieting skills. If the same child were to walk away from the toys, or even just take a deep breath, and then resume playing with the toy, that's a demonstration of good self-quieting skills in action.

Interestingly, the parent who works at and puts in the effort to teach their child self-quieting skills may have some unpleasant times at first but both the parents and the child will reap the benefits for a long, long time. Thus, the parent who is able to put off his own needs, temporarily, stands to benefit a great deal in the long run. On the other hand, the parent who puts his own needs first and does anything that he needs to to reduce his child's frustration, rather than teach his child how to deal with frustration is choosing short-term gain and long-term pain.

An example with an adolescent would be an adolescent who cannot get her stereo to operate properly. Those adolescents without self-quieting skills will usually end up throwing something, kicking, or swearing. While it is obvious that throwing, kicking, or swearing won't help the situation, these teenagers simply don't have the coping skills (this is the way we refer to self-quieting skills in adolescents and adults) that are necessary for dealing with situations that we really don't like.

Some parents have trouble with the idea of letting a child learn how to deal with frustration on his own. They feel almost obligated to help their child in any way they can. I've even heard parents say that it's "cruel" to not help your child to deal with frustration. Given that life for most adults is filled with occasional frustrating situations — situations that are beyond the control of the individual — it makes sense to begin teaching children how to deal with frustration, on their own, whenever they begin to encounter frustrating situations. For those parents who have waited until a child is a teenager without ever helping them to learn self-quieting skills, the entire learning process will be difficult for both parent and child — for the parents because they have to put up with a lot more than they would have had to put up with if they had just done this teaching at an earlier time and for the teenagers because they don't have the skills to cope with the learning process. These are the teenagers who are always blaming someone else for their mistakes or shortcomings. Whether it's their low grades or their poor performance in some other area, the lack of coping skills is a definite handicapping condition.

When and How to Comfort Your Child

There is a real tendency, particularly with young children, to not just comfort them but to attempt, whenever possible, to rectify whatever may have happened to upset the child. For example, for a toddler who falls off of his "big wheel," many parents will not only attempt to comfort the child, they will also try to fix the big wheel, or they will verbally condemn the big wheel for hurting their child. In doing so, the parent prevents the child from learning how to "fix" the situation and, worse than that, the parents give their child the message that they, the parents, are available at any time to fix unpleasant situations. While it's certainly all right for the parent to be available to comfort the child, the parent should allow the child, after he has calmed down, to approach the situation again so that he can do his own rectifying.

The best way to comfort a frustrated child is with physical contact without any verbalizations, or at least without verbalizations that imply that the adult will be able to fix the situation or that the object was responsible for whatever discomfort the child may have experienced. The parent who just holds his child and pats or rubs her back until she has regained her composure, keeps his mouth shut, and then lets the child approach the frustrating situation again is helping the child to learn that when you get frustrated you calm yourself down and then you go right back to the situation that got you frustrated in the first place. Parents who do the fixing for their children are more likely to raise a child who comes to expect someone else to do the fixing and, thus, a child who never learns to do his own fixing.

As children get older, many of the situations that frustrate them or hurt their feelings are also situations where their parents simply are not capable of doing much to "help" the child. For example, for a child in middle school, much of the criticism that they receive is social in nature — not getting invited to an important event or getting teased by a group of other children. In these types of situations, the parents cannot phone the parents of the other children and demand that their child be invited. If they do this they end up subjecting their child to more criticism than he would have gotten in the first place and the child learns nothing of the give and take of social relationships. Nor can they change schools every time that someone is unfairly critical. In fact, I suspect that the biggest difference between children who whine incessantly to their parents and those who do not whine to their parents is not in the amount of criticism the child gets but how well the child can handle the criticism. If they handle criticism well, then they have little to tell their parents about. But, if they have trouble handling criticism, the impression that their parents get is that their child is being subjected to a lot of criticism.

It is much easier to teach a child self-quieting skills than it is to hire an attendant who goes everywhere the child goes to instruct people that your child doesn't handle criticism well and, thus, is entitled to special treatment.

What about Using Distraction or Entertainment instead of Teaching Self-Quieting Skills?

There are many parents who distract their children instead of teaching self-quieting skills. For example, if a child is getting frustrated with her toys, rather than allowing the child to learn how to handle her emotions in that situation, the parent may attempt to substitute another toy, get the child interested in a television show, or try to get her interested in eating something. When this happens, if it happens often, the child is never given the opportunity to learn how to handle the situation by herself.

Like the other examples that I've used under the heading of self-quieting skills, the parents will usually use distraction because they, the parents, feel too uncomfortable if they have to listen to their child crying, fussing, whining, or complaining. The parents really aren't doing what they are doing to benefit their child, they are doing it to prevent their own uncomfortable feelings. Usually parents who are that protective of their own discomfort don't have very good self-quieting or coping skills themselves. From the parents' own experience, the parents have no choice but to assume, as has been the case in their own lives, that the child will remain miserable until another person has helped them. If parents can be helped to understand the importance of self-quieting skills in their children, maybe they can do more to facilitate their child learning these important skills.

Dealing with Emotions

At one time or another, virtually all parents have had to do something to their children that the child doesn't like. Any parent of an adolescent knows how true this statement is. If the parent is constantly looking for the child's approval and wants to make decisions that represent true compromises, in the sense that the solution is something that is equally acceptable to the parent and to the child, then the parents are forsaking their responsibility as role models, mentors, and teachers. It is far more important, and sometimes harder, to raise a child who can exist in the adult world than it is to "keep them happy" in the child world. If a child is denied, through their parents' efforts, the opportunity to experience a wide range of emotions that they are expected to deal with on their own, then the child is forced to enter the adult world without the skills to handle difficult situations that they are bound to encounter.

What about Parents who Don't Have Good Self-Quieting Skills Themselves?

The most obvious examples of parents who don't possess good self-quieting skills are those parents who are impaired — parents with problems with substance abuse or chemical dependency. However, these parents are clearly dysfunctional and have dysfunctional families. They also typically will require therapy, and may experience fragmentation of the family through divorce or intervention of a social agency. The families that are headed by one or both parents who have poor self-quieting skills have the major disadvantage that their children will be seeing and experiencing poor role models. They will be seeing, on almost a daily basis, how NOT to handle frustrating or emotional situations. These children, in turn, must either grow up without these skills or they must find a way to develop them without the assistance of their parents.

I'm convinced that children without good self-quieting skills are much more likely to look for an easy way out than children with good self-quieting skills. If you ever have the opportunity to watch school-age children doing homework or playing a game you will see the big differences that exist between children. Some children get very frustrated with a math problem that they can't figure out, they calm themselves down, and the approach the problem again. Other children get upset with the problem and refuse to continue to do their homework. The child with good self-quieting skills is more likely to get his homework done, is more likely to get it done correctly, and is more likely to be able to face their homework the next time that he is expected to do it. Even the strategy, when taking a test, of skipping the questions that you're not sure of the answers to, until you have had time to go through the entire test and then going back to the more difficult questions requires that the student be able to maintain their "cool" (use their self-quieting skills) so that they don't get upset over the hard questions that they encounter on the first pass through the test. Too often parents will mistake a lack of self-quieting skills for a lack of intelligence. I've heard parents say that their daughter simply can't get math problems correct when the real problem is that their child doesn't have the skills to handle frustrating situations.

There is Nothing Permanent about Self-Quieting Skills

It's good to keep in mind that self-quieting skills aren't necessarily permanent. Just because a young child has good self-quieting skills doesn't mean that he won't lose these skills if his parents or other caregivers handle situations in such a way that they are detrimental to the maintenance of self-quieting skills. In fact, as children encounter frustrating situations as they get older, better self-quieting skills are usually necessary. While a young child with poor self-quieting skills may only be expected to continue to try to ride a big wheel for only a couple more minutes, an older child may

be expected to complete an entire game of Monopoly knowing from at least mid-point in the game that he didn't stand much chance of winning the game. When you see the child who always wants to forfeit the game whenever he isn't winning, you're looking at a child without good self-quieting skills.

Teaching Older Children Self-Quieting Skills

The older a child is, the harder it is to teach them self-quieting skills. Thus, the parent who waits until a child is 10 years of age is bound to face a much more frustrating and demanding task than the parent who started teaching self-quieting skills during infancy and early childhood. The basic process of teaching self-quieting skills is the same regardless of the age of the child — it's just that the level of difficulty changes dramatically as the child gets older.

For over 20 years, numerous practitioners around the country have been advising parents to use *time-out* as a form of discipline for children of all ages. In fact, the range of ages for which time-out is now recommended goes all the way from 7 to 9 months old to 12 to 15 years old. Basically what time-out means is that a child is temporarily restricted from engaging in any of the activities that they would normally have access to. While the length of time varies from professional to professional, the basic principle that a child should be removed from enjoyable activities remains the same. One notable development over the past 10 years has been the emphasis on the use of *time-in* whenever a child is not misbehaving. Time-in is a much broader-reaching strategy than the concept of reinforcement.

Previously, parents were encouraged to *reinforce* good behavior with either some kind of verbal praise or with access to a tangible reward such as watching television or eating something. During the 20 years that time-out has been under development, several points have been made that are worth discussing here in detail.

The effectiveness of time-out depends more upon the activity that is removed, the time-in, than on any characteristic of the time-out.

A research study almost 10 years ago looked at the use of time-out under two very different situations. In one that the researchers referred to as **enhanced time-in**, the parents were instructed to make the time that a child was not in time-out as pleasant as possible. In the second one, that the researchers referred to as *impoverished time-in*, the parents were instructed to make the time that a child was not in time-out very unremarkable. **The researchers discovered that the more enjoyable the time-in was for a child, the more effective the time-outs became.** Thus, the concept of *time-in* was born. Another major finding, and one that was made in our office, was that initially using very brief (two or three seconds of quiet, calm behavior) time-outs was much more effective than the more traditional several minutes of time-out. These two findings will now be discussed in detail.

Time-In

Researchers have repeatedly reported the same finding: the use of any form of punishment can only teach a child what **not** to do. In order to teach a child **what** to do, parents and teachers need to specifically address this issue. Parents should monitor their children's behavior very closely and provide frequent, brief, non-verbal physical contacts whenever the child is not engaging in an undesirable or inappropriate behavior. Thus, if a child is reading, coloring, playing with a brother or sister, or just pensively looking out a window, the parents or caregiver should provide the child with many brief (one or two seconds), nonverbal, physical contacts in the form of physical touches or "love pats." The rationale for making these interactions brief and nonverbal is that this is less likely to disrupt or interrupt what the child is doing. When first starting to do time-in with a child of any age, it is not uncommon for children to be briefly interrupted when a parent comes up to them and touches them on the head or the back. Most children, however, very quickly adapt to these touches and get to the point where they ignore them completely (which is not only desirable but preferable). The fact that these interactions are nonverbal makes them infinitely less disruptive to a child.

Whenever parents see a behavior or a situation that they want to change, they should begin by identifying behaviors that they would like to see in the place of the undesirable behavior. If the desirable behaviors are also incompatible with the behavior that the parents want to work on, all the better. For a period of time, perhaps as long as a couple of days, the parents should begin using time-in prior to ever using any form of discipline. For example, if your child has a long history of being disruptive when you are on the telephone, you should begin your behavior-change strategy by concentrating on the behaviors in which he engages during your phone conversations that you would prefer to see. Throughout the phone call, you should provide a large number of brief, nonverbal, physical contacts whenever your child is not interrupting or annoying you. Only after you have gotten accustomed to providing the brief physical contacts during phone calls should you begin any form of discipline. The same basic strategy should be used for a child's behavior when you have friends over, or when you are trying to talk to your spouse, or when you are in a situation (like shopping in a grocery store) that requires acceptable behavior from your children.

Time-Out

The use of time-out to discourage bad or inappropriate behavior consists of removing the child from the "good things in life" for a period of time. There have been several demonstrations about the use of time-out that are important to summarize here:

- Time-in should always be enriched.
- Short time-outs (five minutes or less) are more effective than long time-outs.
- The explanation of why a child is going to time-out should be brief (preferably no more than three words total)
- The child's release from time-out should only be made when the child is quiet, not after the mere passage of time.
- There should be no verbal contact with a child in time-out under any circumstances.
- There should be no mention or discussion of the reason for the time-out after the time-out is over.
- The sooner a child goes back to time-out for the same offense, the faster he will learn to behave the way you want him to.

When a child is in time-out, he should be able to see you (which means he shouldn't be sent to his room for time-out), he should be able to see that you aren't mad at him, and he should be able to see what he is missing.

The Importance of the Contrast Between Time-In and Time-Out

If the time-in is pleasant enough and the time-outs are dull enough, virtually all children who are emotionally intact will very quickly prefer time-in. Much like a variety of situations that we have been in, the good times are preferable to the bad times.

Relevant examples include the fact that snow skiing is more enjoyable than falling, water skiing is more enjoyable than falling, roller skating is more enjoyable than falling, and ice skating is more enjoyable than falling. In each of these examples, the unpleasant part of the activity is merely the removable of the pleasant part, nothing more. Whenever a parent becomes concerned that time-out isn't working, or isn't as effective as they had hoped it would be, the answer is usually that the time-in with the child isn't rich enough.

What Children Learn from the Use of Time-out

The most important thing that a child learns from the use of time-out is self-quieting skills. If a child must be quiet and calm in order to get up from time-out, and if the child is sent to time-out many times each day, then the child has many opportunities to learn how to self-quiet. While the child is learning how to self-quiet, he is also learning that he would much rather be having a good time than sitting in a chair or on a stairwell doing nothing.

When Time-Out Doesn't Work

There are several things to check when time-out doesn't work. The first is the value of the time-in to the child. If the time-in is not enriched enough for the child, he may prefer going to time-out. The second is how fast the parent is putting the child in time-out. The quicker the child is sent to time-out, the quicker the behavior that got him sent to time-out will begin to weaken. The third is how unemotional the parent is when he sends his child to time-out.

If the child is sent to time-out quickly enough, most parents will have the child in time-out before they become aggravated or annoyed.

Teaching Self-Quieting Skills by Using Time-out

The number of times in one day or one week that a child has to self-quiet is usually not under the control of their parents and, oftentimes, can be very low. For example, the average child only has

7 opportunities in one week to quiet herself down when she goes to bed for the night. However, if the parents are using time-out as their primary form of discipline, then their child may have over 100 opportunities in a week to learn to self-quiet. The nature of self-quieting, as has been discussed at length already, is that it has to be done by the child. Any attempts by the parent to help a child self-quiet will retard the child's learning of self-quieting skills. Thus, for any child who needs to learn self-quieting skills, the more often the child is put into time-out and required to be quiet before her release, the quicker she will learn self-quieting skills. The learning of self-quieting skills is probably, in the long run, substantially more important than whatever the child may be disciplined for.

Specific Situations that Require Self-Quieting Skills

Childhood Fears

There are times for all of us when we have to do something and we get nervous about doing it. Whether it's a noise from the basement, or having to walk to the car from a store after dark, we all have times when we have to discipline ourselves to just go ahead and do something that we don't want to do. Each time we are successful at overcoming such a fear, we have used a skill very similar to self-quieting skills. Almost every child has days when he doesn't want to go to school. Most parents will go ahead, in the absence of definite signs that a child is ill (a fever or vomiting), and make sure that the child goes to school. Some parents, however, feeling sorry for the child or trying to avoid the uncomfortable feelings that come from making their child do something that he doesn't want to do, will allow the child to stay home from school. If this happens a couple of times in a school year, it usually never causes any problems. However, if it begins to follow a pattern, then the child may begin to build very strong feelings of anxiety about going to school. These feelings can get so intense that the child can become physically ill from them.

I have seen children in my office who would get so nervous about going to school that they would vomit at home or in the car on the way to school. Usually, by the time that the children are getting physically ill from their anxiety, the parents get concerned enough to seek professional help in working on the school fears. Most of the time, children who are afraid to go to school in the morning have at least several other situations that they handle in a similar fashion. A recent child in my office was apprehensive about going to school. In talking to his parents, we discovered that he had left Sunday school a couple of times because "he wanted to go home." He had also left a Boy Scout camp two days early because "he wanted to go home." He had also stopped spending nights at friends houses because he didn't want to be away from home. When these kinds of patterns are seen, they usually go back to the same thing — the child doesn't have the skills to manage his own anxiety — he doesn't have self-quieting skills. With younger children, from ages two or three up to five, it is often sufficient, once you have established that such a pattern exists, to simply insist that the child go to such activities and remain at them until they were scheduled to be over. While this may be very difficult on both the parents and on the child, and probably could have been prevented in the first place, the younger children can usually get over it if the parents can tolerate the treatment procedure that requires that the child participate in the activity.

When my son was about to start at his first preschool, at just about three years of age, the preschool where we enrolled him had a requirement that all parents of new enrollees had to attend a parent-teacher meeting. At this meeting, the night before the first day of preschool, the director explained that the next morning all of the parents were required to pull into the parking area, single file, and proceed to the front of the preschool when it was their turn. When they were in the first position in front of the preschool, the director would approach the car and the parent was expected to help the director to extract the child from the car. The director said that we (the parents) could cry if we wanted to but not until we got off of the preschool's property. I'm sure, now, that the reason the director made such a big deal out of the dropoff procedure was that she had had trouble with children in the past. The irony was that, even though I knew that the director was right, both personally and professionally, it didn't keep me from getting a lump in my throat and it didn't keep me from thinking about at least 10 reasons why I didn't have to start my son in preschool that early. With only a couple of exceptions (usually suspected around the time of difficult exams), my son has never had problems going to school in the mornings.

Separation Anxiety

When a child develops a more generalized pattern of having problems separating from his parents, including thinking about the separation when no such separation is imminent, and worrying about what will happen to his parents if they should be separated, we say that the child is exhibiting separation anxiety. Separation anxiety is usually manifested by the child getting extremely emotional whenever he is faced with having to separate from his parents. The reaction that some parents have to their child getting very upset about separating is that they make every attempt to "help" the child to separate. They will hold the child, try to console him, talk sweetly to him, and, generally, confirm any anxiety that the child might have about separating. Often these parents have at least as much discomfort as their child and, when the parent stops to comfort the child, both the parent and the child feel better and they have both made the next separation more difficult. Also, these parents will try to figure out ways of separating less so that they won't have to experience the discomfort of separating. In doing so they just make separation harder for both parent and child.

Some parents do figure out that they must be the ones who separate easily so they can model to their child that separation isn't anything to worry about. If the child has good self-quieting skills, then separating is usually difficult only the first couple of times, then both parent and child can separate very matter-of-factly.

One situation that can complicate separation is with a child who has been very sick and hospitalized in serious or critical condition. The parents are often so relieved that their child survived the terrible ordeal that they aren't worried about how well he or she separates. Thus, over a relatively short time, the parents and the child see again that separation is very difficult. Before anything can be done to help this situation, the parents must be convinced that teaching their child to separate easily is in the child's best interest.

How Can Separation Problems Be Handled?

Once the parents are convinced that separating easily will benefit everyone, the next thing to do is to separate frequently, with the parent at least **acting** like the separation doesn't bother them at all. The more often the parents separate from the child without showing any discomfort, the faster the child will learn to separate easily. I usually recommend that the parents set up several extra separations so that the child gets more practice. They might arrange with a relative or a neighbor to drop off the child, run a short errand, and then come back to pick up the child. If there's a chance that the child will still be fussing when the parent returns, then the parent should call the home where they left the child rather than assume that he has calmed down. When picking up a child who has a difficult time separating, the parents should refrain from heavy displays of emotion. The parent who can separate often and separate unemotionally, can usually teach a young child to do the same within a week. During times when the parent and child are not separating, the parents should not discuss or encourage the child to discuss separation. If you need to watch someone separate easily, watch other parents (who separate easily) to see how they do it. Inevitably, you will see that they just drop the child off in a matter-of-fact manner and drive away. Obviously, you can find a parent who drops their child off with lots of hugs and kisses, and who separates easily — just don't try to fool yourself into thinking that the hugs and kisses came first. Once you learn to separate easily from your child, then you can become more dramatic during the separation because you know that you have taught your child good separation skills.

How Can Problems with Frustration Be Handled?

When children are playing, working on a household chore, or doing homework, and appear to be frustrated, place them in time-out until they self-quiet. This way you can teach them the skills that they need for dealing with frustrating events. You can put your child in time-out whenever he acts out his frustration in a difficult situation. As soon as he has calmed down, his time-out is over and he can go back to the task that was frustrating him. Over time, and through many repetitions, he can learn to self-quiet, which will allow him to complete many difficult tasks that would otherwise have led him to stop because he was frustrated. By the way, there's a chapter, later in this book, on redirecting children while they are at play. Redirecting should not be used as a substitute for self-quieting skills, it should be taught in addition to self-quieting skills.

If children are raised with little or no self-quieting skills, they will probably also have trouble dealing with stress when they get older. The logical extension of self-quieting skills, from a child handling frustration and disappointment well, to an adult who handles stress well, is a natural one. Perhaps the most damaging thing about stress, to an individual, is allowing it to continue. There are adults who can be in very stressful situations for weeks or months at a time, while working right next to another adult, in the same situation, who doesn't find the situation nearly as stressful. The difference between the two is often the one adult's ability to self-quiet. When self-quieting skills are poor or nonexistent, the older an individual is, the more work it will take for him to learn the necessary skills. Sometimes it is advisable for the adult to learn relaxation skills.

Relaxation Skills

One of the benefits of children learning self-quieting skills is that they can use these skills, without even having to think about it, in a number of new or unique situations. For example, children who have learned self-quieting skills at home tend to have fewer problems when they start going to preschool or kindergarten. Although they are consciously doing it, they are able to quiet themselves down even though they may be apprehensive about the new situation that they are in. Typically, a child with good self-quieting skills who is dropped off at preschool may fuss for a couple of minutes and then stop fussing, on his own, and begin participating in the school activities. The same child, without self-quieting skills, would probably end up being "helped" by one of his teachers.

When children simply cannot calm themselves down, it may be necessary for the parents to obtain the services of a competent professional skilled in teaching relaxation skills to children. Perhaps the most common example of this is when a child gets so upset at school or before school that he either almost becomes "unglued" or he becomes physically ill. When children have problems this intense, the time required to teach them self-quieting skills can be greatly shortened by using relaxation procedures. There are many approaches available to teaching children how to relax in response to extreme nervousness. However, if the nervousness is interfering with a child's school attendance, then the parents should seek a competent professional's help rather than try any "home remedies."

Parents interested in learning more about relaxation are referred to the book, *The Relaxation Response* by Dr. Herbert Benson.

Anxiety

What is anxiety and how are children affected by it? The working definition of anxiety is that the person *feeling* the anxiety cannot easily identify the cause of the feeling. A child who is afraid of the dog next door, after having been bitten by the dog, is not anxious, he's smart. Any child who has been bitten by a dog should be nervous around that dog, and perhaps around other dogs. If, however, a child is nervous about going to school, but cannot identify anything in particular about going to school that makes him nervous, he would be considered anxious.

How is anxiety built up? Occasionally children will be so upset by one situation that they will immediately become anxious over it. More often, the child learns the anxiety one step at a time. If a child is nervous about staying overnight at a friend's house and she calls her mother to be rescued, and her mother comes over to pick her up and take her home, the child's anxiety is increased one small notch. Each subsequent time that this child experiences the same situation and the parent rescues her, the anxiety is increased one more notch. Within a fairly short period of time the child's anxiety is such that the child would probably not be able to stay at the friend's house under any circumstance. Although the anxiety grew only one small step each time, with repetition, the anxiety became strong enough to keep the child from actually doing this activity.

The important point is that most children will experience such anxieties, just as most adults will experience an occasional fear of heights or of flying. If the parents are supportive, but do not rescue the child, the child may not feel any better, immediately, but the parents have not done anything to make the fear any worse. After the child has called out to his parents to be rescued on several occasions and the parents have been supportive but refuse to rescue the child, the child will usually learn to deal with the situation without parental help. This is one of those situations like we described above at bedtime — the parents are rescuing the child as much to reduce their own discomfort as they are to reduce their child's discomfort. Unfortunately, while the parents are temporarily reducing their own discomfort, they are also directly contributing to their child's discomfort.

There are some children who, although very convincing about their anxiety, can still be helped by just teaching them self-quieting skills if (and this is sometimes a pretty big "if") the parents can stop themselves from feeding their child's anxiety. And, even if teaching the child self-quieting skills isn't sufficient to eliminate the problem completely, the parents have still taught their child an important skill that they can use for the rest of their life. I'm reminded of several children I've seen who were afraid to go into certain rooms of their house, including their own bedrooms and the bathroom unless they were accompanied by another person. One of my favorites was a five-year-old boy who could not go to sleep unless he had one person (either one of his sisters or his mother or his dad) sitting on his bed, in the dark, with his door open and not talking. This is the way he had gone to sleep for several years. We were able to break this unfortunate habit within one week after we had taught him self-quieting skills during the day. Another child, a seven-year-old boy, had convinced his parents that he could not go to the basement or go upstairs unless someone accompanied him. This child had been in play-therapy for one year, at two sessions a week, to "treat" his anxiety, which, as you may have guessed from what I've said here, only served to strengthen his anxieties. After his parents had taught him self-quieting skills, using frequent time-outs during the day for other situations unrelated to his "fears," it only took a couple of days to get him over his "fears." One day I was talking with his dad on the phone when I overheard the child say to his dad, "Dad, do you think my dog's ears are going to fall off?" His dad immediately said, "time-out," and continued talking to me. Dad told me that he was so pleased because he had never realized how many different small "fears" his son had, nor did he realize that he was, with the best of intentions, encouraging the boys fears by trying to "help" him with them.

Almost any adult who has been troubled by anxiety knows how uncomfortable and sometimes debilitating anxiety can be. If it is possible to teach children self-quieting skills and thereby reduce the child's chances of being bothered by anxiety later, it seems like a very reasonable approach to take.

4

Independent Play

Independent play refers to a child's ability to entertain himself for extended periods of time without any help from an adult. The utility of independent play skills is that they lead directly to such activities as doing homework for extended periods of time, doing seat work at school, working on an independent project for school, and, as an adult, working on projects at home, school, and work. Those adults who are able to concentrate for the three to five hours or more that it takes to complete a home or office project have good independent play skills. Adults who are able to read a book in several sittings were, in all likelihood, children who had good independent play skills.

Characteristic of the adolescent or adult who has poor independent play skills is that they constantly need to be entertained. They're usually great at watching television or enjoying spectator sports — activities that don't really take much concentration or thought. These are the people who can't seem to stand being alone for very long. They will make phone calls or go to someone else's house looking for something to do. They seem to have a television set on or a radio or record/tape player going continuously. The "mall rats" that were popular several years ago (adolescents who frequented shopping malls, often staying for hours at a time) were made up primarily of adolescents who had poor independent play skills.

The best, and perhaps only, indicator we have of how well adjusted a toddler will be as an adolescent is their independent play skills at about four years of age. A toddler with good independent play skills can probably play with toys (watching television doesn't count) for at least one to two hours at a stretch. Many children at four years of age can play for even longer periods of time. As the child gets older, her ability to concentrate and enjoy an activity for a long period of time is simply transferred to other, more age-appropriate activities. This includes children who can play on one activity for 30 to 45 minutes, then switch to another activity, without adult help, for another 30 to 45 minutes. Also, children with good independent play skills can usually play better with other children than children without good independent play skills.

One major advantage of children with good independent play skills is that they can entertain themselves for long periods of time, and this frees the adults around them to do other things besides entertain them. And, for children with good independent play skills, they get two for the price of one — anytime that they are playing they get both the enjoyment of play and the enjoyment of the physical contact with an important adult, a significant other. It seems to be this double gain that works to keep children engaged in independent play. After a child does learn how much enjoyment comes from independent play, the need for input from adults decreases, although you should never take independent play for granted.

Punishment/Discipline

Like the other survival skills that I've already discussed, there is no way that discipline can be used to teach a child independent play skills. All of the punishment in the world probably wouldn't teach a child independent play skills. The only way that a child can be taught independent play skills is through doing it over and over again, gradually increasing the length of time that the child plays, until the child begins to enjoy the play activity. Thus, the child, adolescent, or adult who doesn't have good independent play skills doesn't have the ability to enjoy many of the activities that their same age peers have who do have good independent play skills.

Engagement in Activities

The more children can become engaged in their daily activities, whether it be homework, household chores, or play activities, the more they are going to enjoy the activity and the less likely they are of them getting into trouble. Children who can play for one or two hours alone don't require much adult supervision, nor do they require much discipline. The time a child spends in independent play also allows their primary caregiver more time to get other activities completed. The combination of the child being engaged in activities for long periods and the parent having more time to get their own responsibilities fulfilled leaves both more time for activities they can do together. Building independent play skills in children and adolescents literally has no down side. The better the child's independent play skills, the more time the child and the parent will have for other activities.

Postponing Independent Play Skills

There are many parents who, to make themselves feel better, insist on almost constantly entertaining their children. They're almost like a teacher who makes up lesson plans for each school day. These parents plan activities for their child to account for much of the waking day. Instead of taking the effort to teach the child independent play, and coping with the occasional whining and fussing that children are likely to exhibit while they are learning independent play skills, the parents take the "easy way out" and provide an abnormal amount of structure for the child, which all but guarantees that their child will remain dependent upon them.

Interrupting Independent Play Activities

For years now, verbal praise has really been "in." Parents, teachers, and a variety of professionals have all been told that they have to praise children and adolescents who are doing a nice job. However, as many parents have already discovered the hard way, when they do praise their child, the child often stops doing what she was doing and the parents then need to entertain the child. This is the way that many parents get discouraged from praising their children. The more they praise them, particularly the younger child, the less the child plays independently. As discussed in the chapter on touch, touching is far less likely to distract a child than praise. While it is fine to use praise at the completion of an activity, or when the child stops what she was doing and seeks adult approval, it is far better to use simple touching when the child is actively engaged and concentrating on an activity. The physical touching can gradually be decreased in frequency, over a time period of months, as the child begins to enjoy the activities, and the child continues playing with less of the physical touching.

Does the Activity Make Much Difference?

For the most part, the answer is "no." Whether the child is playing with toys, reading a book, or just sitting and thinking or day dreaming, the fact that the activity can engage the child for long periods of time is the goal that we are looking for. There is almost no way that a parent can predict what independent play activities a child will enjoy. In my opinion, it is far more important for a child to develop independent play activities than to judge the activities they enjoy engaging in by themselves. Once a child finds out, through experience, how much enjoyment they can derive from playing alone, they can extend that skill to other activities.

Independent Play in Infants

Some infants appear to be equipped with good independent play skills in the sense that they don't cry very much and they can concentrate on one thing for several minutes at a time. Rather than take this behavior for granted, or as many parents have been heard to say, "leave him alone, he's quiet," it's almost imperative that the parents do what they can to encourage more independent play activities. There's nothing magic about a child's independent play skills.

If you are constantly entertaining your children, they will look to you for entertainment and may never learn to entertain themselves.

There is a big temptation for new parents to want to entertain their baby during much of the baby's waking hours. In research that has been done with teenage mothers, they typically will carry their infant around with them much more than older mothers will do. The only explanation that I have for this is that teenage mothers have less tolerance for their baby crying than the older mother.

They carry their baby around a lot because they don't know what else to do and because the teenage mothers feel so uncomfortable hearing their babies cry — the stress on them, the teenage mothers, is more than they care to endure.

To encourage independent play in an infant, the adult usually must be physically near the baby, but must not be holding the baby or talking to the baby. When the baby is older than five months of age — old enough that they can handle objects and can look at objects for a period of time — it's possible to begin to encourage independent play. Whenever the baby is engaged in independent play, the adult should make a point of providing their baby with a great deal of brief, nonverbal, physical contact. If the baby's placed on the kitchen floor and is chewing on a teething ring or placing his fingers into his mouth — as long as he is entertaining himself for even a brief period of time — the adult needs to briefly touch the child on the back, head, arms, or legs *without saying one word*. Although these brief touches may distract the child at first, over time these touches will encourage more and more time spent by the child entertaining himself.

Recently, a mother came in for an office visit with a child about one year old who literally cried throughout most of the waking hours of the day — about 11 hours each day. During the entire first office visit the child was on her mother's lap continuously, fussing the whole time. We instructed the mother to use nonverbal physical contact, demonstrated it repeatedly for her, and asked her to demonstrate it for us. We told her that her baby needed as least 500 nonverbal touches in the next week. When the mother returned one week later, the baby never got on her mother's lap and never fussed or whined. She spent the whole time exploring the toys in our office and playing by herself, and, while her mother was talking to us, she would gently move about the office making sure that she touched her child while the child was engaged in an activity. The two most remarkable points about this return office visit, after only one week, were the amount of change in the child (she had gone from almost continuous fussing to almost no fussing at all) and the fact that the mother had actually worn a small bald spot on the back of the baby's head from limiting her touches to exactly the same spot that we had used when we were demonstrating the touching to the mother. (We did, of course, recommend that the mother vary her touching a little more, to spread it out over the baby's upper torso and head!)

Just as many parents do not want to put up with the emotional discomfort that is necessary while their children learn self-quieting skills, encouraging a child to learn independent play skills can produce uncomfortable feelings in parents. When you see a mother or a father who is constantly entertaining their child, almost like it is their job to keep their child entertained, you're seeing a family where the parents are unwittingly teaching their children to be completely dependent upon them in order to avoid uncomfortable feelings. I've seen parents who could not put their baby on the floor because, "He doesn't like to be left alone." This is true even when being alone means that the baby is lying on the floor only a couple of feet from one of his parents. These parents are rarely considering the ramifications of their behavior for their child — they are usually motivated to do what they are doing by their own discomfort. They will often go to great lengths to cover up the fact that they will allow their baby to do whatever he chooses whenever he chooses. They will read to their baby and carry him around the house pointing out everything imaginable from their baby's nose and ears to pictures of family members. Basically these parents will do anything to avoid hearing their baby fuss or cry.

Encouraging Independent Play in Toddlers and Preschoolers

Toddlers are at a perfect age for encouraging independent play activities. As they go about the house, engaging in one activity after another, you must discipline yourself to provide frequent nonverbal, physical contact. There are literally hundreds of activities that toddlers engage in that you can comfortably encourage by your physical contact. Initially, toddlers perform better at household chores as well as play activities if one of their parents does the activity with them. A child who will not play for two minutes with Legos may play for 30 minutes if an adult plays with him. The secret, from the parent's part, is to wait for a moment when your child seems interested in what he is doing and then excuse yourself, saying you'll be right back.

Then leave for about five seconds, just long enough to walk away about 10 feet, turn around, and return to playing with your child. After you've done this about 15 times, your child will, probably for the first time, come to see you as predictable, and will expect you to return. Many parents do just the opposite and then they wonder why their child will not play alone. If you and your child are playing together nicely and you excuse yourself, saying you'll be right back, and then you don't return, your child learns that whenever he plays nicely by himself you leave him. Many parents will leave a child who is playing and, if the child does not protest or follow them, they stay away. Over time, the child learns that when their parent leaves it's for a long time.

After several days of playing with a child several times each day, for about 10 minutes each time, leaving for 5 or 10 seconds at a time, but predictably returning, your child will become less con-

cerned about what you are doing and more interested in what he is doing. Then, when you leave "for a moment" you can be gone for 15 or 20 seconds. If you very gradually extend the length of time that you are gone, your child will gradually learn to enjoy himself, without you necessarily present.

Household chores are handled in a similar fashion. With a toddler, you would start out by doing most chores with them, and, over a period of time, you gradually spend less and less time helping and, within a couple of months, you should find that they can do a remarkably good job at simple tasks like picking up their toys.

Exercise

Because toddlers also spend a lot of time outside, you may have to find some activities that you can do outside. Most parents of toddlers don't get enough exercise themselves. Try going for long walks with your toddler (please don't put them in a stroller — it offers no exercise value to your child). These walks, if you can keep quiet unless you are responding to your child, can be one more opportunity for your child to learn independent play-skills. Begin by helping them a lot with their play and gradually withdrawing your help while they learn to do more and more of the play activity by themselves. It is a good idea to try to find the time everyday to get your child vigorous sustained exercise. Most children and adults will find that they sleep better and generally feel better if they consistently get more exercise. In order for the exercise to be very worthwhile, it must be vigorous. Many parents feel that, because their child runs around their family room, dodging end tables, the child is getting a lot of exercise. Exercise, in order to be of benefit, must result in increased heart rate and increased rate of breathing. Walking fast, swimming, and bicycling are probably the most common exercises that children and adults can do together that are of physical benefit to both age groups.

Encouraging Independent Play in School-age Children

The older a child is before he learns independent play skills, the longer it takes to teach him and usually the harder it is on his parents. A child who is 8 or 10 years old, and who has very poor independent play skills might take 6- or 8-months to learn independent play skills. The basic procedure is the same as with teaching a toddler. The parent has to spend time on a task with the child and then leave for very brief periods of time, and do this frequently, with the idea that the child will come to enjoy the activity and need the assistance of the adult less and less over time. You may have to experiment with several activities, at first, to find one that your son is more interested in than others. Often, though, the school-age child, when left alone to entertain himself, will either call a friend on the phone or try to go to a friend's house to avoid having to entertain himself. As with most other skills, a school-age child doesn't want to spend a long time doing something that he isn't good at, particularly if the activity makes him feel uncomfortable. When my son was about 8 years old, we began building model airplanes together, the kind that are powered by rubber bands. Although it took a fair amount of my time in the beginning, as he found out how much fun he could have with the planes, he got much better at building them by himself, and came to prefer building them by himself rather than having me help him. Later, when he graduated to radio-remote-controlled racing cars, he did almost all of the building by himself. Thus, even though it may have taken me dozens of hours in the beginning, my son learned skills that he ended up using for hundreds of hours. In fact, the last radio-controlled car that he built took him almost 18 hours to finish.

One procedure that works with the school-age child is to discontinue an activity while the child is still enjoying it, before the activity becomes boring or repetitive. An example would be shooting baskets with a basketball. If you shoot baskets with your child for 5 or 10 minutes and then stop before they become bored or says that they don't want to continue, it may be easier to get your child involved in that activity the next time. The biggest mistake is to continue with an activity, stopping only when your child says that they really can't stand to do it anymore. For example, if your son is shooting baskets with dad and has never done this for 15 minutes before without getting bored, it would be a good idea to offer the opportunity to stop before 15 minutes had elapsed. Over a period of time, your child will probably be able to spend increasingly longer periods of time before quitting. Too often, parents will insist that their child finish any activity that she starts, regardless of how much the child wants to quit. It's far more important for your child to quit while he's still enjoying the activity than it is to wait until he can't stand it anymore. Obviously, if you can start to teach independent play with those activities that you strongly suspect that your child enjoys, you stand a better chance of getting them involved in the activity.

Encouraging Independent Play in Adolescents

Teaching independent play to an adolescent is the hardest age at which to start. Adolescents usually have a much better support system than do their younger counterparts, so it's much easier for them to avoid or escape the discomfort that they may feel from entertaining themselves. Where a school-age child might continue with a task during your brief absence, an adolescent will probably try to make a phone call or invite someone over — anything to stop the uncomfortable feelings. For this reason, parents who set out to teach independent play skills to an adolescent had better plan on a lengthy procedure, as well as a procedure that will probably be interrupted many times.

Even though an adolescent may complain bitterly about having to entertain himself, he will benefit from the independent play skills in many different ways, not the least of which is that he learns to concentrate for longer and longer periods of time.

What Role Does Independent Play Have for Adolescents and Adults?

Take the example of two teenagers at a large urban shopping mall. One of the teenagers, the one with good independent play skills, usually goes to the mall with an agenda. They know what they want to accomplish at the mall, have a definite time frame in mind, and know when they want to leave. The teenager without independent play skills has no agenda, no plans, and, if asked what time they think they will be home, they don't know.

How long does it take most children to learn independent play skills? Independent play skills take a long time for children to learn, perhaps as long as four- to six-months, but during this four to sixth month period, you should see steady progress as your child entertains himself for increasingly longer periods of time. And, the entire time that you are teaching your child these skills, you are able to gradually get away for longer and longer periods of time and your child is enjoying what he is doing more and more. Once your child has learned to entertain himself, there is far less need for you to entertain him. The need to discipline him should also decrease because he is doing things that we say are "incompatible" with misbehaving. That is, a child who is enjoying playing with building blocks is far less likely to get into a situation that requires any form of discipline than a child who has nothing to do.

Side Effects of Building Independent Play

Many parents have told me that when they stop what they are doing in order to touch their children, they always interrupt what their children were doing. However, if you will examine what you are doing, you will probably notice that you are talking to your child or doing something else that distracts him. Initially it is hard for many parents to interact with their child without talking, primarily because most of us talk to our children far too much. I can remember several parents, seen in my office, where I have instructed them to use the brief, nonverbal, physical touch while we were talking. The parent will walk over to the child and touch him while saying how nice the child is playing. Then I remind them to do the touching without saying anything and the parent approaches the child, touches him, and whispers something to him about how nicely he is playing. Sometimes it may take five, six, or seven times before the parent can touch their child without talking. What difference does it make how long this process takes as long as you learn how to do it and your child benefits from it?

Similarly, I know parents who have restricted their children's play materials to a family or a playroom that is on another level of the house than the level where the parents usually are. This practice is just asking for it — it makes brief physical contact such a chore that parents are unlikely to do much of it. Try to find storage places close to the areas where you spend most of your time: a drawer or two in the kitchen, a drawer near a work bench, or a toy box near sewing materials. In this way, you will be increasing the likelihood that your child will be playing near you and that you will be in a position to provide a lot of physical contact while they're playing.

The Role of Verbal Praise

Verbal praise obviously has its place in encouraging independent play — usually at natural breaking points or when an activity is **completed**. Other examples would be third-handed compliments. These are compliments that you make to another person at a time when you know that your child can hear you (on the telephone, for example) or compliments that you make to a third person whom you know will relay the compliment to your child. Another kind of praise involves calling a significant other (a grandparent, mommy at work, etc.) and letting your child tell that person what he has just done. Verbal praise is fine when used for finished products, such as a drawing or coloring, but will not help to keep a child on task during the task inself.

Hyperactivity and Independent Play

Many parents provide an atmosphere for their children that would make almost anyone feel hyperactive and then they wonder why their children won't play calmly. While the use of medication and behavior therapy is typically suggested for children with hyperactivity or attention deficit disorder, encouraging independent play is certainly one strategy that is appropriate for children who have trouble concentrating for any length of time. The sections where I have discussed how to encourage independent play for different ages of children address how you can teach independent play skills to a child who you think might tend to be hyperactive. There are some physical changes that you can make that can help until your child learns independent play skills. Turning off disturbing appliances such as TV sets and radios is one way. Discouraging the use of the telephone for periods of time in the evening are another.

Structured Play

Activities. It is important for children to be involved in structured, supervised play activities, such as sports and musical activities. In a research project that was done through my office over a decade ago, we found a striking difference between children who were involved in structured, school-sponsored activities and children who were not. When an adolescent was referred to the juvenile court for a deliquency hearing (in which a judge must decide whether or not to declare a child delinquent), their past history with structured school-related activites was the best predictor of how well they would do with their lives after the court was no longer supervising them. Children who were involved in school-related activities were far less likely to ever be before the juvenile court again, compared to children who weren't involved with any structured, adult-supervised activities.

I don't think that the structured activity was what kept the child from getting into trouble again. Just the opposite. I think that the children who are involved in adult-supervised, school-related activities are less likely to become involved with the juvenile court in the first place and, once having come into contact with the court, they were much more likely to fall back on their existing skills and spend more of their time in structured activities. Children with lots of experience with adult-supervised school-related activities got into these activities because they already had the skills to do well in them. The children without much experience in such activities were more likely to get into trouble again because they didn't have the skills, in the first place, to help them to stay out of trouble.

If a judge or a school principal attempts to change a child who has gotten into trouble, rather than lecturing the child about how the child has "disappointed adults" and how he needs to "get his act together," the adult authority figure should do her best to work with the child's parents to encourage the child to become involved in structured activities. This involvement begins at home.

It's common for some parents to bring work home with them,

such that they spend time during most evenings doing quiet paper work. These parents are not only setting a good example for their children, they are also, by keeping the house quiet and modelling productive use of their time, encouraging their children to follow suit — to get their own priorities and to value those priorities.

In the section of this book on communication, I've made the point that it doesn't do much good to lecture to children about the need for them to change their behavior. Children learn more from watching their parents than from anything that their parents will every say. The same thing is true with independent play activities. From the time your child is a toddler, you can be modelling how to spend productive time alone, accomplishing what you think is important. When both of our children were very young, I spent a lot of time at home writing (and still do). They would often come into my office with a book or with paper and pencil and occupy themselves for anywhere from 20 minutes to two hours. They might, as children do, stop what they were doing to ask me a question or to show me something, but, generally, they were doing something that they had chosen to do and they enjoyed doing it. They didn't have to be disciplined to get their homework done. They had enough time to do their homework, read or play for their own enjoyment, and still had time left for television or Nintendo.™

Children's Schedules

If you look at your children's schedule and you don't see many breaks, then you are not encouraging them to learn to use their time effectively. If your child has one-adult supervised activity after school each week, and if he uses the rest of his time effectively, then you don't have much to worry about. I can remember many evenings, including on weekends, when one of my children has been in their room for several hours. When I've asked them what they were doing, they would either say, "Nothing," or they'd say that they were just "straightening their rooms." This kind of activity can't take place if there's no time for it. It can't take place if you are constantly driving your child from one activity to another.

Cordless Phones and Independent Play

One of the most useful recent advances is the cordless phone. Countless parents, over the years, have told me that their children seem to be at their worst when they, the parents, are on the phone. Yet, if you spend a minute to analyze this situation, you probably ignore any good behavior from your child so that you can talk on the phone. Yet, the instant your child gets into trouble or does something that you dislike, you will interrupt your phone call to discipline him. Basically, what this situation boils down to is that you don't have the option of not being interrupted. You can choose to be interrupted by touching your child or by disciplining him. You don't have the option of uninterrupted phone calls. However, if you use the cordless phone so that you can do lots of touching while you continue with your phone call, you will soon find that your child is playing better while you are on the phone and you don't need to do as much touching. One caution here — when your touching during phone calls gets below a certain critical point,

you will find that you start getting interrupted again by inappropriate behaviors. These interruptions should tell you that you need to increase your touching again.

If you don't have a cordless phone then consider either getting a long cord for your phone or put a modular outlet for your phone closer to where you usually spend your time and where your children often spend their play time.

Changing the Environment Around to Facilitate the Touching

Another very simple technique to facilitate touching is to either move the chair you are in closer to the child so that the touching is easier or to place your child's toys near you to make the touching easier to do. If mom is finishing up in the kitchen and dad is drinking a cup of coffee at the kitchen table (what a sexist example!), dad can do frequent touches with his child if he can reach him. If dad must get up each time and walk over to the child, then dad gets tired of getting up and down so much and the child may get distracted by all of the motion. With just a slight shift in the placement of dad's chair, or a move to a chair closer to your child, the touching is greatly facilitated.

Using Habit-Pairing as an Aid

Some parents, with the best of intentions, just find it difficult to provide the amount of the physical contact that their children need in order to learn independent play. To overcome this difficulty, you can pair an established habit with the habit that you want to learn. For example, if you routinely walk through your family room or kitchen to get to your washer and dryer, you can try to remind yourself to touch your children every time you head for the utility area. This is similar to the strategy that many of us have used over the years of placing a medication that we previously haven't had to take next to our toothbrush. In that way, every time we pick up our toothbrush, we're reminded to take our medication. If you are a smoker, you can place a small note between the cigarette pack and the cellophane cover to remind you to touch your children. Similarly, you might place a small note next to the diet drinks. Any such strategy depends upon the soundness of the original habit and the cleverness of your pairing. This habit pairing may take one or two weeks to get established, but from then on you may find that the combination of the habit getting better developed and the pleasure that you derive from your child's new independent play skills may be enough to keep you going.

Another strategy is to use a kitchen timer. Just set the timer for four or five minutes, and if you haven't touched your child by the time the timer rings, go do so and reset the timer. If you do remember to touch your child before the timer sounds, then reset the timer. Over a couple of days, you may very well find that both you and your children are doing much better.

Looking for Playmates and Baby-sitters with Good Independent Play Skills

If your daughter only plays with other children who need to be constantly entertained, she will not be learning good independent play skills. In fact, one characteristic of children with good independent play skills is that, when two or three of them are playing together, they will often end up each playing with something alone. This doesn't mean that they don't have good social skills, it just means that they enjoy playing by themselves as much as they enjoy playing with other children.

Some baby-sitters are excellent at getting their homework done while they are babysitting. This usually doesn't mean that they are neglecting the child. In fact, teenagers with poor independent play skills probably never get any homework done while they are babysitting because they get distracted by the babysitting and never get started on their homework. Other baby-sitters seem to need to be entertaining the child constantly. This isn't really as laudable as it might appear. If a child is playing quietly on the floor in the family room, it's silly for the baby-sitter, or the parent for that matter, to interrupt the child. Better to provide the child with a lot of nonverbal physical contact and keep the verbal interaction to a minimum.

What about Parents Who Are Runners— Who Have No Independent Play Skills Themselves?

Many parents lack independent play skills themselves. These are the parents who watch a lot of TV, the parents who always have an errand to run. Years ago I used to tease a friend of mine that if you asked his daughter what her room at home looked like she would describe the inside of the family automobile. She had spent so much time in the car with her mother, running one errand after another, that the skills that she was learning were mainly connected with running errands. She probably never put a puzzle together that had more than ten pieces because she was never at the puzzle long enough to do so. Another friend of mine had a son who could put together puzzles of hundreds of pieces at the age of about 4 or 5 years old. Although he may have had an average I.Q., he had developed excellent independent play skills. Average children with good independent play skills can often accomplish much more than a really bright child who has poor independent play skills.

Adults Without Independent Play Skills

One of the characteristics of adults with poor independent play skills is that they don't usually like to be alone and they don't like peace and quiet. When left alone, they will almost inevitably have a television set on or a radio blaring. Some adults are almost compulsive telephoners. Because they don't have the skills to use their own time effectively, they will call someone else and, in doing so, they end up with something to do — they talk to their friend. These are the type of adults who should not get themselves into positions where they have projects that must be completed without any supervision or interim deadlines because they won't usually be able to get the job done on time.

Just because a parent doesn't have good independent play skills doesn't mean that they can't teach their child to have them. It just means that the parent is going to have to put more effort into it than a parent with good independent play skills.

What about Families with Several Children?

Whether you have one child or five, they all need to learn independent play skills. Granted there is opportunity to develop independent play skills with a houseful of siblings, the need for these skills when a child gets out on her own is the same whether she has ten siblings or no siblings.

5

Redirecting Your Child

There are many times when parents are tempted to redirect, distract, or otherwise "help" their children. Redirection, with a child who already has good self-quieting skills and independent play skills, does give the parents more options and, when used correctly over a period of time, teaches children one more way to deal with situations that they find boring, uncomfortable, frustrating, or just down-right unpleasant.

When Should I Redirect My Child?

There are two answers to the "when" question. One deals with the age at which you begin to use redirection and the other with the issue of "when," in a given situation, the parent should use redirection. From a chronological standpoint, the earlier a child learns self-quieting skills, the earlier the parent can begin to use redirecting. To use redirection prior to a child having self-quieting skills is a mistake. So, for an 18-month-old child, who already is good at self-quieting, redirecting is a logical thing to do. For a 10-year-old with poor self-quieting skills, the parent needs to work on self-quieting skills prior to giving much consideration to redirecting.

Within a given situation, the earlier that you try redirecting, the easier it will be on both you and on your child. Given a child who already has good self-quieting skills, it's a good idea to try redirecting them occasionally in order to teach them one more option for dealing with their own emotions. Thus, when your child seems to be getting frustrated, it's a good idea to try to redirect him as soon as you can. In fact, if you wait too long to try redirection, you'll probably just end up having to place him in time-out to give him the opportunity to cool off or settle down. When he does cool off, then you can choose whether you redirect him or encourage him to go back to the activity that got to him in the first place. If you see your child is starting to get frustrated with a task or a chore, you can suggest that he deal with something else for a while and come back to the original task later. If your child is already upset about the task that he is working on, then self-quieting is the logical step to take prior to any attempt to redirect. Thus, the only time that redirecting really has much chance of working is if you can catch them early and redirect them before their emotion begins to build.

What Are the Best Situations to Begin Redirecting With?

Concrete situations, such as chores or homework, are the easiest to deal with first. They're easiest because you can tell how much progress your child is making (or not making, as the case may be). If you can see that your son is getting frustrated with his math homework, and you know that he also has some homework from world history, then you can suggest that he take a breather from his math and work on his world history homework. More abstract situations, like when your child is trying to convince you to let him do something that you do not want him to do, are more difficult to assess and are less likely to be helped by redirection.

What Is Wrong With Using Redirecting Almost Exclusively?

Many parents, usually the ones who don't appreciate the enormous importance that self-quieting skills play later on in life, seem to like to redirect their children, particularly when they see that their child is beginning to get frustrated. This is often a mistake if the child doesn't already have self-quieting skills. In fact, for the child who doesn't have good self-quieting skills, the parent who always wants to redirect is probably reacting as much to their own emotion, in the sense of wanting to redirect their child so that they, the parent, won't have to deal with the negative emotions that they see about to erupt from their child. I've seen this situation so many times with young children. If a child is playing with a toy and the toy isn't doing what it's supposed to do, and the child begins to get upset about it, the parent immediately jumps in and tries to get the child interested in some other activity.

For the child who doesn't self-quiet easily this only perpetuates the child's problem. But, in order for you to teach your child the self-quieting skills, you might have to put up with a number of unpleasant time-outs and you may have a tendency to try to avoid that situation if at all possible. If you would encourage the self-quieting skills first, and, after your child has gotten good at self-quieting, then begin to use redirecting, you would be helping your child to learn to use a variety of strategies that can be adapted to many other situations for years to come.

Redirecting an Infant

Just as soon as your baby has learned to self-quiet, you can begin to use redirection. If your baby is crawling around the family room and he comes in contact with an electrical cord, he should be immediately placed in time-out, rather than redirecting him. After he gets good about quieting down when he's in time-out, then you can begin to use redirection. For example, for a child who already has good self-quieting skills, if he's playing with a toy and he seems to be getting bored with it, it's a good idea to redirect him to another toy before he gets upset with the first one. However, you have to be careful that you aren't monitoring the child so carefully that you aren't allowing him or her to learn about their world and the frustration that's an integral part of it. I have seen too many mothers who behaved more like they were attendants than parents. They are constantly monitoring their child and trying to head off any situation they can before their child experiences any frustration. Although, superficially, it looks like they are doing a wonderful job with their baby (he hardly fusses at all!), the baby wouldn't be able to function if he didn't have his mommy

watching his every move, waiting with the vigilance of a predator
to pick up any pending signs of distress. Better to teach the child
how to deal with the distress, then work on redirecting.

Redirecting a Toddler

If a toddler is riding a tricycle around in the basement and he
or she encounters an obstacle, and begins to fuss, don't move the
obstacle. Wait at least until the toddler stops fussing and,
preferably, give him or her some time to solve their own dilemma.
Some intelligence tests for young children include a component
where the child must be able to figure out their way around an
obstacle. Without the parent's help, many children won't do well
on these kind of tasks. Now, after your child has been riding the
bike around the basement for 10 or 15 minutes, it's not a bad idea
to redirect to another activity, not to save them from the frustration
of hitting obstacles, but to teach the child to switch from one
activity to another while still having a good time.

Redirecting a School Age Child

A classic example, and one that many teachers will try to get their students to use, is to skip over test questions that they don't know the answer to almost immediately. If a child spends too much time on one question, without figuring out what the answer is, he or she loses two ways. The child gets a little demoralized by not being able to answer the question and has less time left to finish the rest of the test. If, on the other hand, the child has both good self-quieting skills and good skills for redirecting, they can stop themselves from getting upset immediately and skip over the hard questions. I can remember, in college, sometimes answering only 5 or 10 questions the first time through an important final exam. However, this fast pass through the first time served two functions. One, it let me know that there were a number of questions that I knew the answers to and, two, it gave me more time to work on the questions that I found more difficult.

Modelling Redirection

I have had numerous times around my own children when I have used redirection myself and pointed out to them why I was doing it. Once, when I was trying to develop some Polaroid slide film, I used up several packages (at over $10 a package) before it occurred to me that there was something wrong with the developer. Instead of trying to figure out what was wrong with the developer, I told my son that I was going to go upstairs and work on something else for a while and come back to the developer later. When he asked me why I didn't want to work on the developer then, I told him that I wanted to be able to approach it when I was fresh. If children can learn this strategy, both by practicing it with our help, and watching us use it to our own advantage, they will have one more skill that they can use for years to come.

Where does Redirection Fit Into the Big Picture?

Redirection is one skill that children can use, after they have self-quieted, that can allow them to approach a difficult situation in a calm, matter-of-fact manner. However, it's a skill that when used by a well-intentioned parent, in order to avoid emotional situations, can actually retard a child's learning self-quieting skills.

6

Cognitive Development

How much of what a child does is determined by their genetic endowment and how much is determined by the environment in which they are raised? This is an age-old question and one where the answer changes from time to time. I'm not sure whether the answer changes because we learn more about children or because we cycle through different fads. I am sure that there is a definite and unchangeable part that child development plays in the life of every child.

Each child is born with a genetic endowment that will determine the range within which the environment can operate, given, of course, that no environment event, such as an injury or a serious illness, forever changes what the genetic endowment would otherwise have allowed. With regard to a child's intelligence, genetics determines the range within which the environment can have an impact. A child may be born with an I.Q. that will be somewhere in the normal range (from an I.Q. of 90 up to 110). If the environment is optimal, the education appropriate, both in terms of when and how it impacts the child, and the child normal in terms of his learning, then his I.Q. will probably be closer to the 110 mark. If, in contrast, the environment is full of chaos, the education barely adequate, and the child subjected to numerous events that are not conducive to learning, then his I.Q. will probably be closer to the 90 mark.

If the parents provide a child with extensive tutoring, and enrich the child's life with a multitude of cultural and religious events, the child's I.Q. range will not be appreciably affected, and probably cannot be raised above the level determined by his genetic endowment. Nor will the I.Q. be appreciably affected by the school that the child attends or the teachers that the child is assigned. Sure, some teachers are better than others and some schools are better than others, but, over the long run, one teacher or one school is not going to be the critical element in the academic development of a child.

Cognitive Development in Children

The development of the skills necessary for abstract reasoning plays a very important role in the development of a child. Children who are seven years of age or younger are at the "preabstract level of cognitive development," which means that they are unable to deal with abstractions such as reasoning. If a parent tells her three-year-old daughter, Jennifer, not to go into the street because there are cars and she might get hit and be hurt, Jennifer may be perfectly capable of repeating such an instruction back to her mom and dad, saying, "Jennifer, street, hurt" but that is where her ability ends. It is extremely unlikely that she will be able to actually do what her parent instructs her to do. If Jennifer's parents want her to not play in the street, they will need to teach Jennifer to stay out of the street — not just talk to Jennifer about it.

Implications for Parents

Because reasoning with young children doesn't work, it usually results in repeating the instruction over and over again, using threats and nagging, such as "If I have to tell you one more time," or "If I've told you once, I've told you a hundred times," or "How many times do I have to tell you?" Her parent ends up telling her the same thing over and over again because Jennifer is unable to comply with the instruction, due to her level of cognitive development. When Mom gives the same instruction repeatedly, she begins to believe that Jennifer is openly defying her, and Mom begins to feel frustrated and/or angry.

Implications for Children

From a child's perspective, when their parent repeats the same warning or reprimand over and over again, the child begins to feel that Mom does not like her because she gives threats and yells at her. Over time, repeated, unsuccessful, attempts to reason with a child can result in lowering the child's self-esteem. As this process goes on, day after day, the parent gets more and more frustrated and the child develops a very poor self-image. The perpetual warning system, as I've come to call repeatedly warning children, doesn't do any good for either the parents or the child. It just leads to frustration and hurt.

How Do Children Learn?

If you, as a parent, are interested in getting your children to behave in a certain way, without encountering undue frustration and without putting down your child, then you have no choice but to face the facts and use what we know about children's learning to accomplish your goal. Children, like adults, learn through repetition. They must have the opportunity to practice the same thing over and over again.

Learning how to ski (water or snow) provides an excellent example of the important role that practice plays in learning how to do something. Ski instructors will typically spend a relatively brief period of time explaining how to put on the skis and take them off. Then it's off to the water or the slopes to practice. When you first begin to ski, you will usually find that you fall a lot — sometimes it seems like you spend most of your time falling. All of the lectures in the world wouldn't help you to learn how to ski. You just have to practice and practice and practice until you learn how to do it. If someone yells at you a lot and continually reprimands you for not skiing properly, you'll just get increasingly more uptight without learning anything about skiing — except, perhaps, that getting yelled at just makes skiing less enjoyable.

If you can think about teaching a child to behave like you were teaching them how to ski, you would probably do things very differently. I know some very accomplished skiers, who can do some pretty amazing things on skis, but none of them learned how to ski from a lecture. They learned how to ski by practicing skiing. Children will learn how you want them to behave by behaving. There aren't any shortcuts. Surely, if there were a simpler way to teach children how to behave appropriately, someone would have discovered it by now. If nagging, reprimanding, and warning worked, you would see it in every educational institution in the country.

If Jennifer needs to be gentle with her new baby sister, she must be shown this lesson over and over again. Every time that Jennifer plays nicely with her sister, regardless of what she's doing, mom needs to provide Jennifer with a great deal of brief, nonverbal physical contact. Every time that Jennifer is rough with the baby or does something that her mom doesn't want her to do with the baby, she needs to be disciplined in an unemotional way. After Jennifer has experienced twenty or thirty interactions with her sister, with some resulting in pleasant physical contact and some resulting in discipline, Jennifer will learn from the contrast "how to" play with her sister.

Parents cannot tell small children once not to do something and realistically expect the child never to do it again. Parents need to understand that teaching involves many repetitions before something is learned and that children must do something both the right way and the wrong way many times before they learn to do it right consistently. Rather than becoming frustrated because learning takes place over a long period of time, parents should understand that they are in the process of teaching their child important skills. The more times the child can experience the contrast between what happens when something is done the right way and when it is done the wrong way, the quicker and more thoroughly the child will learn what the right way is.

I have heard many parents say that they can't wait until their children are old enough to "reason with" as though the day this happens will forever change their lives. Ironically, virtually every one of us has had numerous opportunities to let another adult know how much we would like to see them change a particular behavior, but, after numerous discussions, we have all seen that there is little, if any, change in behavior. Just because adults have the ability to reason things through doesn't mean that they are going to use this ability.

What are the implications of this for child rearing? Simple. The less time and effort that you spend trying to reason with your children, the happier you and your child are going to be. Just as you hate to be constantly reminded of your mistakes by your spouse or significant other, so does your child hate to be reminded of her mistakes.

There's an old expression that parents will often resort to saying to their children out of frustration, **"If you don't have anything nice to say, then don't say anything at all."** This expression also applies to you.

At What Age Can Parents Begin to Try to Reason with their Children?

This is really a loaded question. Most of the times that parents want to reason with their child it is because they are frustrated. It's not because they really believe that their child will change from their reasoning attempts, as much as it is that the parents want their child to know how much frustration they are causing their parents. A number of years ago there was a parent education program in many cities around the United States that held the basic notion that parents were supposed to let their children know how their misbehavior affected their parents. Even though this program really wasn't very helpful to parents in terms of making their children behave better, many parents liked it because it gave them license to nag their children as much as they wanted. The formal parenting program didn't ever suggest that parents should nag their children or that nagging would make the child behave any better. Its main drawing power was that it appealed to parents who were going to give their children a "piece of their mind" anyway and now the parents could do it with a clear conscience.

Nagging is Not an Educational Process, It Is a Form of Harassment.

If nagging, warning, threatening, and yelling at your children won't do you any good, in terms of getting your children to behave the way you'd like them to, then what can you do? That's what the rest of this book is all about.

7

Self-Esteem

Most of the time, we don't discuss self-esteem until we're concerned that a child or adolescent has low self-esteem. In actuality, we have some very good ideas about what contributes to self-esteem and what detracts from it. You can draw an analogy between self-esteem and a savings account. The nice things and the accomplishments that happen to children or adolescents contribute to their self-esteem. These include pleasant remarks, success at things that are important to them, and pleasant contact with significant people in the child's life. The unpleasant things that happen to a child are subtracted from their self-esteem — things like nagging, warnings, reprimands, and other verbal "putdowns," as well as a wide variety of failures including not being chosen for a team sport, bad grades, and disputes with significant others. What is left is their level of self-esteem — add in all of the pleasant interactions, substract the unpleasant, and what's left is an indication of your child's self-esteem.

Additions

Every time that you have a pleasant interaction with your child, you are helping to build his self-esteem. Fortunately, they don't have to excel in order to make deposits to their self-esteem account. I know that it sounds corny, but every "kind word" is an addition to self-esteem. The easiest and most convenient way to build self-esteem is by touching your child. Over an extended period of time, these touches — that all count as deposits to his account — will help to offset any subtractions that you make.

Most forms of verbal praise also add to a child's self-esteem, as long as the praise is realistic in the eyes of the child. If you have an argument with your child and, shortly thereafter you praise them for some job well done, they are more likely to remember the argument than the verbal praise. There's also a form of praise, that I refer to as "third-hand compliments" that is usually appreciated by a child, often more than direct praise. If you are talking to your spouse or one of your parents, and you mention something that your daughter did that was particularly nice, within hearing distance of your daughter, she'll appreciate the compliment. Or, if you say something to your spouse who later says something to your daughter about your compliment, she'll take that as a compliment too.

Children also need to develop one or two areas of competence. It really doesn't matter whether this competence is in sports, academic pursuits, social interactions, or in isolated activities that the child engages in at home (such as computer programming).

The more proficient children become at an activity, with the appropriate recognition from the significant persons in their lives, the more it contributes to their self-esteem. Unfortunately, there's no way that we can choose which activities our child will excel in, nor can we choose what level of excellence our child considers excelling. One of the beauties of this way of looking at self-esteem enhancement is that our children can get twice the benefit from their activities. If your child is reading a book and you provide them with a lot of brief, nonverbal, physical contact, they are getting two for the price of one. The child is getting the enjoyment out of reading and the enjoyment out of the attention that you are giving them. Even a game, like Monopoly, can serve as an opportunity to provide lots of these "love pats." Whether your child wins or loses, and whether they play well or not, they still get the love pats.

When Do We Start Building Self-Esteem?

We usually can't tell much about a child's self-esteem before they are about six years of age, mainly because they don't have the verbal skills to convey how they feel. We begin to build up or tear down a child's self-esteem by the time they have receptive comprehension. That is, we begin to have an effect on self-esteem when the child knows that you are talking about them and they have a general idea of what you are saying. An infant playing on the floor, a toddler coloring, a school-age child reading a book, or a teenager working on a homework assignment can be given a great deal of brief, nonverbal, physical contact.

There have been some interesting research studies done that have shown that when you pet your dog, both the dog's blood pressure and yours will usually decrease. I'm fascinated why no one has done the same type of research with parents giving physical contact to their children. When a child gets hurt, either physically or emotionally, the best form of comfort that parents can give is physical comfort. Not only does this comfort your child for that moment, but it also lets him know that you were willing to take the time to comfort him — it lets him know that you care. Some research has been done on the effects of physical contact on babies born prematurely, by Dr. Tiffany Fields that showed dramatic effects on weight gain in babies who were given several "infant massages" each day. Thus, the brief, nonverbal, physical contact should be started during infancy and continued through adolescence.

Subtractions

I don't know one adult who likes being read the "riot act" or being "chewed out," but I know many, many parents who do this to their children with the mistaken notion that the child will benefit from such interactions. If you look at any of the popular books on getting along or succeeding in business, from *How to Win Friends and Influence People* to *The One Minute Manager*, you'll notice that they all say basically the same thing — don't put down your employees and make every attempt to build your employees up. Isn't a child at least as important as an employee?

A child's self-esteem also takes a bit of a beating when he fails at something that was important to him. If he or she is in school, or at some after-school activity and they are the last one picked for a team, they will feel hurt. If the child disappoints you, his or her feelings may be hurt, whether you intended it or not. Thus, when the child fails at something, he or she has to bear the burden of knowing that **he or she** failed and that they disappointed you. If you have made a practice of providing your child with a great deal of physical contact, regardless of whether or not they have accomplished something or succeeded at something, they will come to appreciate your unending support and, with time, they will develop the kind of self-esteem that it takes to embark on new activities knowing that you will be supportive, not judgmental.

School Performance as It Relates to Self-Esteem

Some parents say that their child's school performance is very important to them. For others, the performance is very important but the parents try to play it down. Few parents can honestly say that their child's school performance doesn't matter to them at all.

I have long been an advocate of trying to ignore poor performance and to be attentive to good performance. If your daughter brings home 10 graded assignments at one time, and six or seven are As or Bs, and the rest Cs or Ds, you should show enthusiasm for the good grades and try to ignore the not-so-good grades. This may be hard for you to do, but you really don't have much choice. To go over all of the papers and "put him or her through the mill" for every low grade is just telling them that you are disappointed with them. I know that some people say that you should criticize the behavior and not them, but I also know that children are smart enough to know that when you are criticizing their behavior they know that you are unhappy with them.

Building Self-Esteem

Our job, as parents, is to help to build our children's self-esteem up enough that no one else can take it down. I'm not talking about their proficiency at any one task. Children can be very proficient at a sport and still feel like they haven't done well enough if one or both of their parents are constantly pushing them to perform better or at a higher level.

A child gets more out of a good performance with lots of recognition from their parents than he or she gets from a great performance with no recognition from their parents. One potential problem with verbal praise is that we always run the risk of saying the wrong thing, particularly when we are talking to an adolescent. You might think that you are really going out of your way to say something pleasant but your son gets angry because of what you said. If you use physical contact as your primary form of praise and acceptance, you don't have to worry whether you say the right thing or not.

There are also times when your children will do something that they know was "stupid" and they don't want to hear from you that you understand, or that you have done stupid things before. They need your support, not necessarily your wisdom. Provide them with that physical support and you don't have to worry about what you say. Talking, in cases like that one I'm describing, is simply a parents' way of dealing with their own uncomfortable feelings. As I said earlier, unless your child or adolescent happens to feel like talking about the same thing that you want to talk about, you run the risk of talking about something that they don't want to hear. You, in turn, may misinterpret their rejection of what you said as being argumentative. Nice deal for your son! First he does something stupid, then you tell him that it wasn't so bad and he gets irritated because he didn't even want to be reminded about what he did. Then, because he gets irritated with what you said, you feel as though he's getting smart with you. What started out with the best of intentions on his part didn't go the way that he wanted. Then, what started out with the best of intentions on your part doesn't go the way you wanted it to. In the end you wind up saying things to your son that you don't mean — all piled on top of good intentions. If you can get accustomed to using more physical contact and less verbal praise, you will be more appreciated and you run less of a risk of getting into trouble because you said the wrong thing.

If your children go on to college or into the work force with high self-esteem, they will probably be able to withstand most of the abuse that naturally occurs in these settings. Because there is virtually no way to avoid the failure, criticism, ridicule, and harrassment that occurs to all of us at one time or another, the only option available to us, for our children, is to do everything we can to teach our children adaptive skills and competencies and to raise their self-esteem as high as we can so that no single failure or disappointment will be enough to really disturb them. They need to know that, regardless of their performance at any given time or on any given activity, they are always welcome to return to us for comfort and support.

8

Parent Coping Skills

Although discussion about teaching children self-quieting skills and independent play skills is important, if parents don't have the skills to contain themselves and to discipline themselves to encourage the development of these skills in their children, then their children will probably never learn these skills.

While it is vitally important for you to be able to encourage your children to develop self-quieting and independent play skills, you have to have reasonable coping skills yourself if you are to be able to carry through. The term *coping skills* is used here to refer to your ability to maintain your own composure in the face of unpleasantness from your children.

One interesting observation that I've made is that children, unlike their adult counterparts, do not have to think about self-quieting strategies. If a child learns self-quieting skills, then when he or she is faced with a difficult or frustrating situation, they can settle down almost automatically. That is, they can do it without even thinking about it. Adults, on the other hand, can only settle down automatically or without thinking if they learned these settling skills when they were children. All of the adults that I know who have learned the skills for coping with difficult situations have had to learn a two-step process. First, they have had to learn how to identify a difficult situation and how to prevent themselves from reacting to the situation immediately because when they do react immediately, they react emotionally and they do not cope well. Second, once they have identified that they are in a difficult situation they must consciously think about the coping strategy before they can successfully implement it. The advantage, then, in teaching a child self-quieting skills, is that he won't have to even think about them when he encounters a difficult situation, whereas an adult in the same situation would probably have to deal with the situation very carefully and thoughtfully.

While you can minimize the effort that it takes on your part to help your children develop these skills, there are still times when you need to be able to step back and allow your child to fuss until he self-quiets. By getting a baby on a sleep/wake schedule and by getting him a lot of exercise each day you can make it easier for him to develop self-transition skills at bedtime. However, there really isn't any way to make this process completely painless for you. While this sounds relatively easy to do, in real life it is sometimes difficult. For example, when a baby is self-quieting at bedtime, or a teenager is obviously frustrated with their math homework, it may take a great effort on your part to leave your child alone until he or she quiets down. Particularly with older children, there is a tremendous temptation to try to tell them, over and over again, that all they need to do is calm down. The realization that they would have already calmed down if they only had the skills to do so is not something that we normally think about when our children are getting on our nerves.

When your child is upset about something that has happened to him or her, the immediate temptation is to do whatever you can to reduce his distress. The hurt that we feel, as parents, is a significant motivator. We have feelings just like our children do and we want to protect them as much as possible. If we help our children to quiet down and relax, it makes us feel better immediately, because it temporarily relieves our distress, even though it keeps our child from learning an important skill. It's easy to tell ourselves that "this time I'm going to give in but tomorrow, when I have more patience, I'll be able to follow through properly." Unfortunately, that tomorrow never comes. It may be difficult and anxiety provoking for us to stand by while one of our children learns to self-quiet but in the long run it's going to be worth it. One strategy that we, as parents, can use to help us get through these hard times has to do with what we say or think to ourselves — our

self-talk. Self-talking can take two distinctly different paths. One is *hurtful thoughts* and the other is *helpful thoughts*. I'll discuss each one at some length.

Hurtful Thoughts

There are many times when we start saying things to ourselves that makes it easier for us to do things that we know aren't good for our children. Hurtful self-thoughts refers to things that we say to ourselves that not only do not make the situation any easier, they frequently make the situation worse. These hurtful self-thoughts are perfectly normal parental reactions to uncomfortable situations, but they can and do interfere with us doing what we know, intellectually, is the right thing. An example of a hurtful self-thought would be a parent who has placed a baby in his crib for his afternoon nap and the baby starts fussing immediately. Many parents start to try to figure out "what's wrong" with their baby. Did I place him in the crib wrong? Is he still hungry? Does he need more attention? Does his diaper need changing? While all of these examples of self-thoughts sound reasonable, they are less reasonable when you consider that you just had the baby in your arms less than one minute earlier, right after feeding him, playing with him, and changing his diaper. Yet this type of self-thoughts can make us doubt our competence as parents — all because we don't have a baby who can go to sleep the instant that he is placed in his crib.

The problem with such hurtful thoughts is that they more or less give you, as a parent, permission to allow your child to do something that you know is not in your child's own best interest. Parents learn hurtful thoughts much like they would learn any other maladaptive behaviors. The situation of getting your own child to engage in a behavior that, although ultimately beneficial to the child, produces immediate discomfort to you and to your child, is similar to many other situations that adults face where escaping the situation is, in and of itself, a rewarding experience. Thus, the tense parent who is attempting to get a child to do something that the child doesn't want to do, is likely to feel a tremendous sense of relief when they give up on getting the child to do it. Over time, these episodes of giving up and feeling immediate relief end up reinforcing the parent for their hurtful thoughts. It may take a fair amount of soul-searching and a fair amount of time before you can identify when you are engaging in hurtful self-thoughts. As you encounter situations that you don't handle particularly well, and after the situation is over and you are less emotional, you need to analyze the situation in an attempt to identify where your hurtful thoughts occurred and what helpful thoughts you might have been able to substitute. So, if you have been getting your 5-year-old to go to sleep at night by lying down with them on their bed, you need to think about what goes through your mind at the time that you are deciding to lie down with them. You may be thinking that "I can't stand it when they cry at bedtime. I don't want him to grow up hating to go to bed at night." The irony with these kinds of self-thoughts is that you are doing exactly the opposite of what you are trying to convince yourself is going on. By lying down with your child you are actually keeping him from learning the self-quieting skills that could be beneficial to him for the rest of his life. I'm reminded of our family trips to Disneyland and Disney World when our children were younger. Because our children were young, and because it was quite expensive, we didn't want to get two separate motel rooms. But, when it was time for our children to go to bed, they went to bed, even though we did not go to bed with them and, because they had such good self-quieting skills, they could go to sleep on a bed in the same room where their mother and I were watching television, eating a late night snack, and talking. If we were following the same procedures as those parents who have children without good self-quieting skills, we would have had to skip the snacks, television, and conversation and go to sleep with the children.

Actually, because we knew that our children had good skills for going to sleep at night, we did not have to even think about them at their bedtime. We just naturally told them it was time to go to sleep. We didn't have to go through some long, drawn-out rationale about how important it was to get a good night's sleep because tomorrow was going to be a big day. We just asked them to go to sleep and they did.

For parents who experience hurtful thoughts in a situation like I've just described, they must first be able to identify their own hurtful thoughts before they can do anything to improve the situation. They have to learn to challenge their own thoughts. When you do first begin to challenge your own thoughts, you are going to come up with nice, slick answers because that's the very nature of hurtful thoughts — they have to be nice and slick or we wouldn't believe them. In fact, for parents who didn't have good self-quieting skills, they will often learn hurtful self-thoughts almost as a mechanism to protect themselves, in order to feel more comfortable.

Helpful Thoughts

Parents who already have good self-quieting skills probably already have helpful thoughts. If they are in a position where they have to teach their children to be able to go to sleep by themselves, they usually don't have much trouble coming up with a reason or a rationalization for doing so. I used to be surprised by the kinds of self-statements some parents — the ones with good self-quieting skills — would make.

A mother with five young children, said her daughter insisted that someone lie down with her at bedtime. The mom said that, "the only way her daughter was ever going to learn how to go to sleep is if she let her do it on her own. If I go in and help I'm only going to make things worse." For this mother, the helpful thoughts came very easily. She didn't need any help with learning them, they were almost automatic.

Parents in uncomfortable situations who are thinking hurtful thoughts need to be able to think "helpful" thoughts. First, parents need to learn how to stop the hurtful thoughts. Then, and only then, can they substitute a helpful thought. The first step in dealing with unpleasant feelings and hurtful thoughts is being able to recognize when they are occuring and stopping or discontinuing the hurtful thoughts as soon as possible. Usually this is easier if we begin by practicing stopping our thought processes in less intense or less emotionally ladened situations. For example, while it may simply be too difficult to catch ourselves in a confrontation with our children, we may be able to look for a situation in business or in traffic where we can practice. If someone is driving entirely too close to the back of your car, and you notice yourself getting angry with him, hurtful thoughts are very common. Examples would be, "If I have to stop fast, he's going to run right into the back of my car." Or, "I ought to slam on my brakes and show that jerk a real lesson." The first thing that anyone has to do in this situation, and many people already know how to do it, is to catch yourself engaging in hurtful thoughts and force yourself to STOP. This might consist of challenging our hurtful thoughts (in the sense of intellectually questioning the wiseness of our hurtful thoughts), or merely stopping our hurtful thoughts long enough (usually only one or two seconds) to think about alternatives. With a one- or two-second break in our thinking, it is much easier to then challenge the hurtful thoughts. For example, instead of thinking, "He's got no right to drive that close to the back of my car," which is kind of silly anyway since he's already driving that close to the back of my car, we can say, "Given that he's already chosen to drive that close to me, what ARE my options?" The immediate option, and the one that most reasonable people will take, is to conclude that moving out of his way is the safest thing to do. Once the "jerk" has passed us, there is very little chance that he will drive into the back of our car.

It is through exercising such cognitive actions, such cognitive coping skills, in less emotional situations, that we begin the process of identifying exactly when we are engaging in hurtful thoughts and disciplining ourselves to substitute more helpful thoughts. Virtually all of us engage in hurtful thoughts some of the time, so the exercise is hardly ever a waste of time. Once we can get some experience at identifying when we are engaging in hurtful thoughts, we can begin the process of challenging these hurtful thoughts and acknowledging their very existence. Some parents may want to begin with benign situations. For example, you might begin with where the paper carrier left your newspaper. It's one thing to say that he has no right to throw it into the middle of your front yard, when he "knows you want it up on the front stoop", it's another thing to acknowledge that the paper is already in the front yard. Since few people have ever run into serious problems with newspaper location, this might be an easy place for some individuals to begin.

It is only after we can identify our feelings about a situation that we can begin a process called: **STOP, CHALLENGE, ACT.** This refers to our forcing ourselves to **STOP** the hurtful thoughts, **CHALLENGE** them with at least one or two of the alternative thoughts that are possible and less hurtful, and **ACT** upon them by changing which one of the alternatives available to us we elect to think. The beautiful thing about our individual thinking is that no one has access to our thoughts and we can think anything that we want and choose to think about.

Some gimmicks that have been used by individuals to get themselves the one or two seconds that they need to think include a rubber band, carried around the wrist and snapped across the soft inner side whenever we begin to notice ourselves thinking hurtful thoughts. Often just the very brief snap of the rubber band is enough to give us a second or two to think. A second gimmick is the use of what is called *thought stopping*. Thought stopping refers to our intentional substitution of a thought that, in comparison to our hurtful thought, carries much more emotion, only of a completely different kind. For example, if you can remember a time when you saw an automobile accident immediately after it happened and you were completely filled with emotion, as soon as you catch yourself thinking hurtful thoughts, you can switch to thinking about the automobile accident. Such a process frequently gives us a second or two to pause and reflect, during which it is easy to conclude that the present situation is no where near as serious to us as the automobile accident was to the individuals involved. Whatever we do, we have to have a strategy that we can implement to help us to identify hurtful thoughts and to substitute helpful thoughts. When you get proficient at identifying and challenging hurtful thoughts and acting upon them in more helpful ways, dealing with your children should become easier. Some parents have learned to carry a 3" x 5" in paper card with them with some helpful thought on it. That way all they have to do is read the helpful thought each time that they begin to experience an emotion that may interfere with their ability to handle a situation in a way that their child will benefit instead of in a way that the parent will experience less discomfort.

Infant Example

If you put your infant to bed awake but drowsy, and let her cry for one or two minutes until she self-quiets, you will probably have hurtful thoughts initially. Thoughts such as, "She's afraid of the dark." Or "I'm afraid that she thinks that I abandoned her." If you stop to think about it for a couple of seconds, it will probably occur to you that she's too little to even know what "abandon" means. Rather, she's probably just grown accustomed to having you help her go to sleep at night and she misses that help. The helpful thought that you can substitute would be something like, "I know that she may be unhappy for a couple of nights, but I can stand it. Once she learns self-quieting skills, she can use them the rest of her life." You have to discipline yourself to be able to put up with your own discomfort in order that your daughter may learn important survival skills. Of course, my preference would be to have you begin to teach your infant self-quieting skills during the day, when situations aren't as emotionally charged as they are at bedtime and when you aren't as tired as you are at your child's bedtime. If your baby begins to fuss because they can't reach a ball that's on the floor immediately in front of their hand, even if you have hurtful thoughts, they aren't going to be as bad as the ones that you would have at your child's bedtime. It's much easier to say to yourself, "He's just got to learn that if he wants the ball, he's going to have to lean or stretch forward enough to get to it." You're not likely to think that he's fussing about the ball because he's afraid that you abandoned him. Similarly, if you begin to put your baby to bed for an afternoon nap, when it's still light outside, you're not likely to be thinking, "She's afraid of the dark," because it isn't dark yet. After you have successfully put your baby to bed for naps for many days, and your baby has been successful at settling down and falling off to sleep on her own, then you will be better able to think self-thoughts that are helpful.

Toddler Example

When children get into the terrible twos, it's common for them to get quite unpleasant when they don't get their own way. Yet, in our lives we experience not getting our own way all of the time. When your toddler wants something, for example, at the check-out stand at the grocery store, and he begins to complain and fuss the instant you say, "No," you may have some hurtful thoughts such as, "He'll probably never forget this day as long as he lives. He may carry these scars with him for the rest of his life." Instead of trying to challenge these thoughts in the middle of a grocery store, you might resolve to work on your daughter's inability to accept the word "No" and what it means when you are at home and you don't feel nearly as much social pressure. Only after you have mastered numerous situations at home should you even attempt to challenge your hurtful thoughts in a public place like the grocery store. Challenging these thoughts is easy. Do you remember (**not** "Were you told"), do you actually remember whether you were breast fed or bottle fed? Wore cloth diapers or disposable diapers? The point here is that children don't remember an unpleasant but otherwise unremarkable moment just because they didn't get their way. A helpful thought might be, "My son may misbehave in public and I may feel embarassed, but I can stand it because I know that he will benefit from it." Again, you have to learn to discipline yourself to be able to put up with your own discomfort in order that your son may learn important survival skills.

School-age Example

With school-age children, social and academic examples probably occur with the most frequency.

Parents will often let their children poke and stall around until the last second and then they allow themselves to get angry. Hurtful self-thoughts at that time might be something like, "He knows that he's got to be out of here is two minutes and he's intentionally stalling." In actual fact, most children don't have the same concept of time that their parents do. They usually don't understand the importance of getting things done in a timely fashion, nor do they care. A more helpful self-thought could be, "If I'm ever going to expect him to get ready in time, I'm going to have to teach him how to do things in a timely fashion." Then (and this is the hard part) you need to find times during the week when you can have your son practice getting something done in a timely fashion. An example that occurs all of the time is the child who isn't getting ready for school on time. Instead of working on this during the precious few minutes that we have in the morning, it's better to work on it after school, during the evening, or on the weekend, when their poking and stalling won't really bother us. So, if you want your daughter in bed by 9:00 p.m., ask her to get ready at about 8:00 p.m. If she hasn't started getting ready within about 2 seconds, send her to time-out. As soon as she's quieted herself down in time-out, ask her again if she will please get ready for bed. Again, give her about 2 seconds to get started and then send her back to time out. After about 30 minutes of this routine, don't be at all surprised if she gets ready when you ask her to. You may have to follow this example every night for a week or two, but, if you can keep your cool and take the time to teach her how to get ready in a timely fashion, you and your daughter will reap the benefits for years to come. Incidentally, while your daughter is sitting in time-out because she didn't get ready for bed when you asked her to, you can be going ahead and eating the snack that she would have gotten if she had just gone ahead and gotten ready for bed. You could also begin reading a bedtime story to a daughter who isn't there. The point here is that she must be able to see what she is missing — to see what she would have been doing if only she had done what you asked her to do.

Adolescent Example

A fairly common comment for a teenager to make is that she will be the only one at her school who doesn't get to go to a particular social function. Such a statement takes it for granted that it is good for her to do what every other teenager is doing and leaves it up to you, her parents, to make her look and feel different. Thus, if you don't allow her to go you are intentionally forcing her to be different, as though you had no concern for how she fits in with her friends. The stage has been set for your self-thoughts. "Do I want my daughter to be the odd one — the only one who doesn't get to go?", "What right do I have to be so severe with my daughter?" It's almost as though teenagers know how to make their parents doubt their motives — they know how to get their parents to begin having hurtful self-thoughts.

As a parent, a helpful thought might be, "I know that she would like to go but I also know that there won't be adequate supervision" or "I know that her feelings will be hurt if she doesn't get to go but she'll get over it". A more general response might be that "I know that I have to make some decisions that my daughter doesn't like, and decisions that might make me feel uncomfortable, but that's my responsibility as her parent."

But, you have to have enough control over your own emotions that you give yourself the necessary time to think about and weigh your options before you have to commit yourself to one plan of action. You may need to write out a statement such as, "She may take a long time to learns these things now, but once learned she can use them for the rest of her life," on the blank 3" x 5" inch card. Each time that you feel yourself starting to get upset because she "knows that you want her to get ready faster," you can take out your card and remind yourself that this is a teaching process, not something that happens in a couple of minutes. After your daughter has had 30 or 40 opportunities to get ready in time, and she stalls long enough to watch a fun activity instead of particpate in it, she will probably "learn" how to move faster when you ask her to.

Learning Takes Practice

Learning coping skills takes practice just as learning almost any other skill takes practice. Although most people cannot improve their coping skills overnight, they can, with practice, learn how to recognize when they are not coping well with a situation, as well as learn how to better cope with situations. The rationale that I described of starting out with a situation that is easier for you is based upon one very important fact — you will be much better able to teach your child self-quieting skills if you have some ability to quiet yourself. Parents may be the only people that we expect to be really good at a skill before they have had enough time and practice to learn it. We would never expect a child to be able to play baseball with an adult, nor would we expect a beginning photographer to be able to take the same kind of pictures that an adult is able to take. Yet, when it comes to dealing with emotional situations, we, as parents, often expect ourselves to be able to handle almost anything.

Drs. Jay and Harriet Barrish, in their book, *Managing Parental Anger,* suggest the use of worksheets to help parents to identify their hurtful self-thoughts as well as to help them to learn a more helpful self-thought. On these sheets, they list the following:

1. What happened? (the situation that occurred)
2. What you thought to yourself that didn't help
3. What your behavior looked like
4. What could you have thought to yourself?
5. What could your behavior have looked like?
6. How could your child have handled the situation differently?

I add one more question to their list. **Is there an easier situation where I could begin teaching my child the same lesson?** So, if we go back to the infant situation where we had an infant who wasn't able to fall asleep alone at night, my first question would be, "Is there a less emotional situation where I could apply these same questions and help my daughter to learn the skills that she needs to have?" The answer as I've already stated is, "Yes, I can teach her self-quieting skills during the day." Then, during the daytime situation, you can go through the questions that the Barrishes suggest that you ask yourself. If your infant is reaching out for a ball, cannot quite grasp it, and begins fussing, and you go over and hand the ball to him or her, the answers would be: **What did I think to myself?** They can't reach the ball . They are only going to get frustrated and cry. Besides, I have the time and the energy to help them. Why shouldn't I? My behavior, in turn, looked like that of a parent who was unable to put up with their own discomfort so that their child could learn an important self-quieting skill as well as the important skill of reaching out to get something that they want. **What could I have thought to myself?** "They are never going to learn how to reach for things unless I help them. Sure, I may feel a little uncomfortable, but I'm willing to experience a little discomfort so that my child can learn some very important skills." **What would my behavior look like then?** Like a responsible parent. A parent who is able to put up with my own discomfort so that my baby can learn. **How would my child react differently to this change in the way that I handled the situation?** Instead of my helping them while they only learned to cry when they wanted something, I taught them to be a little more independent. I helped to teach them the satisfaction that only comes from accomplishing something on your own.

Changing the Things I Can Change

Many parents can overwhelm themselves just thinking about all that they have to do with their children. Yet, if they take what need to be done one step at a time, they can probably accomplish all that needs to be done. This book has been written with particular emphasis on the major developmental levels of your child. You can and should read ahead so that you can see why I consider self-quieting skills and independent play skills so important. However, when you are implementing the strategies discussed in this book, just concentrate on those that apply to the age of your child.

If it takes you several weeks or even several months, to bring about the changes in your behavior that will provide long term benefits to your child, the time that you put into it will be well worth the effort.

Parents and Stepparents Helping Each Other

There is no reason to be embarrassed when you find that you don't handle all situations as well as you would have liked. There will be times when you simply cannot handle your children. If you have a spouse or a significant other who can take over for you, that would be real nice. However, if you are alone and you know that you are having trouble implementing the strategies that I've discussed here, remember that it is the long term that we're concerned about, much more so than today's behavior or tomorrow's behavior.

Learning Parent Coping Skills

Although it may take time and effort to learn coping skills that are useful to you when you are dealing with your child(ren), the effort that you put into it will be well worth it. Even though the need for good coping skills is less when you have an infant, that is exactly why this is a great time to begin learning the self-discipline (the helpful thoughts) that you will need when your children get older. If you know before you have children, or when your children are very young that you tend to have a bad temper, get started on learning coping skills before you need them—learn how to use them in situations at work or with other family members. Usually, if you can discipline yourself to use helpful thoughts instead of hurtful thoughts, you can transfer this learning to situations that involve your children. Consider taking a class or reading a book on cognitive behavioral modification, stress management, or on relaxation. Begin learning how to keep your emotions in check before you have the added responsibility of having to deal with the behavior of one of your children—chances are you'll never regret the effort that you put into learning these skills. And, if you find out that it is much more difficult to keep your emotions in check than you thought it would be, you have time to get professional help, and benefit from it, before your children become more challenging.

And, if you have children who are already 8 or 10 years old, remember that any effort that you can put into teaching them the skills that I've discussed herein should be well worth your while.

Concluding Remarks

You have now been provided with examples of skills that are very important for adults that can be taught during childhood, how you can encourage their development, and what an important role they play in the daily lives of children and adults. I've discussed the uncomfortable feelings that you may have to endure as you watch your children develop them. And, I've discussed some of the strategies that you can use, yourself, to make watching your children develop them a slightly easier task, emotionally, for you, and some strategies to make it easier for you to cope with your responsibility as a parent.

When children have both self-quieting skills and independent play skills and when they know how and when to redirect themselves, they appear to learn faster, even though they aren't any more intelligent than their peers; they are better at sharing and caring, even though they aren't more understanding than their peers; they are better at getting things done than their peers; and they appear to be under less stress, even though they are probably under the same amount of stress as their peers.

Children who are well behaved, children who go to bed easily, children who are toilet trained without undue stress on either parent or child, and children who play well and share well with other children, are typically children who have good self-quieting skills and good independent play skills.

Perhaps the most important thing to remember about children with good self-quieting skills and good independent play skills is that they have the skills they need to survive as adults.

They can take the stress that they are going to encounter better than most of their peers. They can adapt to situations better than most of their peers. They are less likely to have stress related problems. They are prepared to be children of the stress-related '90s.

Much of what has been written about child rearing has been as if there were no tomorrow when, in fact, whether you like it or not, the parenting that you do will last a lifetime. If your child learns to deal with the everyday problems that they will encounter as a child, they will have the skills to deal with the everyday problems that they will encounter as adults. If, on the other hand, your child learns how to be dependent upon adults, learns how to fuss and whine in order to get their way, learns to throw tantrums when they don't like what's going on, they will be poorly equipped to deal with the problems that they are sure to encounter as adults.

Suggested Additional Readings

Barrish, I.J., and Barrish, H.H. 1989. *Surviving and Enjoying Your Adolescent.* Kansas City, MO: Westport Publishers , Inc.

An excellent resource book for parents of normal teenagers. Discusses and provides detailed suggestions for the day-to-day problems of living with a teenager.

Barrish, H.H., and Barrish, I.J. 1989. *Managing and Understanding Parental Anger.* Kansas City, MO: Westport Publishers, Inc.

Describes how we, as parents, allow our emotions to lead us instead of the other way around. Provides some very good suggestions on keeping our emotions in line.

Benson, Herbert, and Klipper, Miriam Z. 1976. *The Relaxation Response.* New York: Avon.

The most accurate, popular, easy-to-read book on relaxation.

Brazelton, T. Berry. 1973. *Neonatal Behavioral Assessment Scale.* Philadelphia: Lippincott.

A very technical manual that describes how to administer the Neonatal Behavioral Assessment Scale. Provides details on testing an infant's self-quieting skills.

Sammons, W. A. H. 1989. *The Self-Calmed Baby: A Liberating Approach to Parenting Your Infant.* Boston: Little, Brown.

Schmitt, Barton. 1987, 1991. *Your Child's Health.* New York: Bantam Books.

One of the most useful and authoritative pediatric guidebooks for parents. Covers all of the common illnesses that children might get.

Spock, Benjamin M. 1976. *Baby and Child Care.* Revised Edition (Illus.) New York: Pocket Books.

Still my favorite.

Weissbluth, Marc. 1987 *Healthy Sleep Habits, Healthy Child.* New York: Fawcett Columbine.

A leading researcher and clinician with children's sleep problems, Dr. Weissbluth provides many valuable suggestions on preventing sleep problems and dealing with problems after they have occurred.

Moe, Michelle. Kisses from Heaven Infant Massage Kit. Lee's Summit, Missouri: Kisses from Heaven, Inc. 1997.

Summary Handouts

At the back of this book, you'll find summaries of many of the procedures or recommendations that are discussed in the text, as well as some that are of related interest.

These pages may be photocopied so you don't have to tear them out of the book.

These summaries are designed to be used after you have read the book. If you rely upon the summaries without reading the book, you probably won't get the full benefit of the book.

 **Time-In: Two-Handed**

Time-in is used by parents to let their child know that they are loved and valued. Time-in consists of briefly and gently touching your child's arm, leg, head, or shoulder for 2-3 seconds, without saying a word. This gentle touching is done repeatedly throughout the day, not because the child has earned it, but because the child is treasured. Time-in is used along with any rewards that parents already do with their child for good behavior.

Time-in is done without speaking to minimize the chance that you will disrupt your child's on-going activity. Verbal comments are much more likely to interrupt and distract the child. Time-in is touching, not speaking. Whether your child is 3 months, 3 years, or 13 years old, you are encouraged to repeatedly touch them for 2-3 seconds while they are engaging in any behavior that is acceptable to you. Parents can nonverbally let their child know that they are loved when the child is doing any of the following: sitting, watching TV, coloring, building with blocks, or just looking out the window.

Parents have a strong tendency to want to talk to their child each time that they touch their child's arm, leg, head, or shoulder. We recommend that one hand be used for touching your child and the other be gently placed over your mouth to help to control the tendency to talk too much. Two-handed time-in helps parents stop their habit of speaking while briefly touching their child.

There are, of course, naturally occurring breaks in a child's activity when praise is appropriate and not disruptive. For example, if your child has colored a picture and brings the finished drawing to show to you, some type of verbal praise would be appropriate. However, the verbal praise at the completion of the activity is no substitute for the brief physical contacts during the activity.

© Robert Ward, Matthew Hoag, and Edward Christophersen, 1997.

Infant Massage

There is no question that touch, and massage in particular, provides the opportunity for parents to spend some close, relaxing time with their baby. After a bath and right before sleep are good times to gently stroke your baby. You want to use the pads of your fingers and apply pressure to avoid tickling, which is unpleasant to the very young infant.

1. Begin the massage with your baby lying on their back with you positioned in front of them.
2. Start with gentle strokes to their face and head, being careful to avoid the fontanels (the two soft spots on the top of his head).
3. Move down the torso and rub their arms and legs.
4. You can also turn them on their stomach to give a back massage. Move from broad, sweeping strokes to finer finger movements, and end with an easy rocking motion.
5. About 10 minutes, two to three times each day is enough.
6. Continue with the infant massage for at least two to three weeks.

For a thorough review of how to massage your infant, refer to Michelle Moe's "Kisses from Heaven Infant Massage Kit." In it, she includes a Manual, a videotape, a small pillow to place under the baby's neck during the massage, and a container of massage oil that is suitable for an infant.

DISCIPLINE FOR TODDLERS

Effective discipline of toddlers requires three major components.

First, the amount of time-in must be adequate. (See the handout on Time-In and the handout on Time-In: Two-Handed.)

Second, any instructions must be given in an effective manner. (See the handout on Effective Instruction Giving.)

Third, and least important, the discipline must consist primarily of removing the time-in. What makes time-out so effective is the absence of time-in, rather than the "punishment" of having to stay in a particular place, such as a chair or the child's room.

There are several important rules for time-out.
1. Time-out must be done immediately. Even a wait of one minute can markedly reduce the effectiveness of time-out.

2. Time-out must be initiated as unemotionally as possible. We usually suggest that the caregiver use only three words, such as: "time-out hitting," or "time-out whining."

3. Once the time-out is initiated, there should be no communication of any kind about or to the toddler who is in time-out. This means no reminders, no repri-mands, and no hints about how to get out of time-out -- either during time-out or after time-out.

4. As soon as the toddler is calm and collected for two or three seconds, the caregiver can either say "OK," "time-in," or "all right," or she can merely resume interacting with the child.

5. Time-out should be repeated as often as neccessary. A child who is "timed-out" for whining can be timed-out for whining 30 times in a row if he whines every time the time-in is resumed. It is this element -- the child actually practic-ing how to calm himself down -- that make the time-out process effective for teaching children self-calming skills. There is virtually nothing that a caregiver can do can "help" a child calm herself down.

6. If there is more than one caregiver, they should focus their efforts on teaching the child skills, not teaching each other. Thus, if a child is whining and her mother does not initiate a time-out, the father (or any significant other) should initiate the time-out. Similarly, if the child is playing nicely but the mother is ignoring her, the significant other should provide the time-in, not remind the mother to provide the time-in.

Preventing Excessive Crying with your Infant

Initially, virtually all babies cry a lot. However, there are specific things that parents can do to help to reduce the amount of crying that their babies do and, in turn, to make the first few months a more pleasant experience for both parents and infant. Here are some suggestions according to the age of your infant.

Newborn

Establish Consistent Routines

If you can discipline yourself to develop consistent routines for such caregiving as diapering, bathing, and shampooing your baby, you will probably find that you get more relaxed while your baby fusses less.

Love Pats

When your baby is quietly watching what you are doing or entertaining his or herself by sucking on their hand or fingers, give many brief, physical "love pats " without saying a word. Try to make sure that you give them 50 to 100 such pats every day. Over time, they will learn skills for keeping busy.

Brief, Boring, Night Feedings

When feeding your baby at night, leave the lights off and don't talk. You can very gently caress or hold him or her, just refrain from providing any more stimulation than is necessitated by a feeding.

Quiet Time

Try to have time every day when all noisy appliances, such as TVs and radios are off, and you aren't talking on the phone or talking to your baby—just plain quiet time.

Two Months of Age

Pick Up Cute Babies

When your baby awakens from a nap or from their night's sleep, they will begin babbling and cooing instead of crying immediately. Make sure that you are up in time to pick up your baby before the crying actually starts. Before about 8 weeks of age, the baby's transition from sleeping to crying is simply too short for you to expect to get to him or her. After 8 to 10 weeks of age, they will wake up and make cute noises before they begin to cry. If you can consistently get to them before they cry, they will learn that you will take care of them when they babble and coo and will have no need to cry every time they awaken.

Put your Baby to Bed Awake But Drowsy

In the newborn period, babies will typically fall asleep while nursing. After 8 to 10 weeks of age you will probably notice that your baby will finish nursing without falling asleep. If you will put your baby to bed awake but drowsy, and be sure that there are several things in the crib that your baby can look at and later reach out to, they will learn "transition skills" to help them in the transition from the wake state to the sleep state. These transition skills can be helpful to your baby for years to come. Babies with good self-quieting skills will usually learn these transition skills quicker and earlier than babies with poor self-quieting skills.

Testing your Infant's Self-Quieting Skills

In order to test your baby's self-quieting skills, you will have to pick a time during the first month of life when your baby is happy, content, and sleeping. This test measures the number of activities on your part that are necessary to interfere with this fussing and allow your baby to move to a quieter state. Wake your baby up with either a loud clap of your hands, above the crib or bassinet, or by moving him around enough to get him crying. As soon as he has been fussing or crying for 15 seconds, progress through the following steps:

1. ALONE. Leave him or her completely alone for a full two minutes to see if he or she is capable of quieting. Although the two minutes may seem like an eternity, wait the full time. He or she is considered to have self-quieting skills if they quiet for at least 5 seconds. If he or she is still crying at the end of two minutes, then progress to the next step.

2. PARENT'S FACE ALONE. Lean over your baby so that your face is about 10 inches from their face. If your baby is still crying at the end of 30 seconds, then progress to the next step.

3. PARENT'S VOICE AND FACE ALONE. While leaning over your baby, talk to them in a normal voice (both voice level and intonation). If your baby is still crying at the end of 30 seconds, then progress to the next step.

4. HAND ON BELLY STEADILY. While continuing to look at your baby, talk softly, and place your hand on his or her belly steadily. If your baby is still crying at the end of 30 seconds, then progress to the next step.

5. HAND ON BELLY AND RESTRAINING ONE OR BOTH ARMS. While continuing to look at your baby, talk softly and hold one or both of their hands firmly against their chest. If he is still crying at the end of 30 seconds, then progress to the next step.

6. PICKING UP AND HOLDING. Pick up your infant and hold snuggly against your chest while continuing to look at him or her and talk to him or her. If your baby is still crying at the end of 30 seconds, then progress to the next step.

7. HOLDING AND ROCKING. While continuing to talk to your baby softly, begin rocking him back and forth. If he or she is still crying at the end of 30 seconds, then progress to the next step.

8. DRESSING, HOLDING IN ARMS, AND ROCKING. Pick your baby up and place him or her on a receiving blanket. Wrap the blanket snugly around your baby and rock gently while talking to him or her softly. If your baby is still crying at end of the 30 seconds, then progress to the next step.

9. PACIFIER OR FINGER TO SUCK IN ADDITION TO DRESSING, HOLDING, AND ROCKING. With your baby still wrapped in the receiving blanket, offer him or her your finger or a pacifier while continuing to rock him gently and talking to him or her softly.

10. NOT CONSOLABLE. If none of the nine steps above work, you have a baby who is very difficult to console. Before jumping to any drastic conclusions, be sure to repeat the test at least two additional times, on different days. If you still apparently have a baby who is very difficult to console, make sure to mention it to your pediatrician at the first well baby visit.

Teaching Self-Quieting Skills to Toddlers

You should discipline yourself to take advantage of every naturally occurring opportunity to teach your child self-quieting skills. If your child comes up to you with their feelings hurt, or after falling off their tricycle, try to refrain from saying anything. Rather, hold them against you, without saying a word, while you rub their back and pat them. In this way, they will learn that you are a great source of comfort when they need you. But, they will also learn that you don't quiet them down—they are responsible for quieting themselves down.

Using time-outs for discipline is another way of teaching toddlers self-quieting skills. Every time that you send your toddler to time-out and they quiet down, they are learning self-quieting skills. While there may only be one or two opportunities in a day to let a child naturally quiet himself down, using time-outs can create many opportunities for the same skills to be practiced.

If you keep reminding your toddler that they must be quiet when they are in time-out, they will never have the opportunity to self-quiet. They must learn to quiet down without any help from you whatsoever. That means that, if they are having a horrendous tantrum—you must let them quiet down. To comfort a child who is having a tantrum only encourages them to have more.

Remember, the more opportunities, and the closer the opportunities are to each other, the quicker your toddler will learn self-quieting.

ENCOURAGING THE DEVELOPMENT
OF SELF-CALMING SKILLS

Although the disciplinary procedure referred to as "time-out" has been around for a long time, many parents have found that it, in their words, "doesn't work." One reason that we believe that it does not work is that parents are using time-out as a method to force their children to change their behavior.

The reason that many children "misbehave," is that they do not have the skills for dealing with situations that they do not like. When children do not get their way, they do not have the skills for self-quieting, or, as it applies to adults, "coping skills." We sometimes see this referred to as "anger control skills," and these children are often said to have "bad tempers," to be "strong willed," or to be "difficult children."

Many parents, with the best of intentions, will put a great deal of effort into trying to convince their children, using lectures, explanations and reasoning, into behaving differently. When this fails, they move into what we refer to as their "coercive mode." That is, they are going to get the child to behave the way they want them to behave no matter what it takes. This often leads to direct confrontations that are unpleasant for both parent and child and usually accomplishes nothing beneficial.

For these reasons, we are now recommending that parents begin giving their children the opportunity to learn "self-calming skills." There are several major components to teaching these skills:

1. Reduce nagging, lecturing, threatening, and warnings as much as possible - preferably eliminate them completely.

2. Provide your child with a great deal of brief, non-verbal, time-in.

3. Take advantage of any naturally occurring opportunities to allow your child to self-quiet. Look for situations where you know that the only thing that has happened is that your child is frustrated, when you know he hasn't been hurt and he's not afraid. For example, if your son is playing with blocks and the blocks fall over and he starts to whine or to cry. Leave him alone until he quiets himself down for about 2-3 seconds. Then, immediately start paying attention to him, preferably without providing any reassurance and without any verbal commentary. Over time, you will see that your son gets better at self-calming.

4. You can also use time-outs to encourage the development of self-calming skills. State briefly, in just three words, in a non-emotional tone of voice "...calm

down." This is usually in the form of "Interrupting, calm down" or "Whining, calm down." For example, if you have been providing your child with a lot of brief, non-verbal physical contact when they were not bothering you, then, when they do interrupt you, all you say is "Interrupting, clam down." Then it is extremely important that you ignore your child until he is quiet, or he has regained his composure. During these "calm down periods," you should refrain from all warnings, naggings, reminders of what he did or did not do. Basically, you should strive to completely ignore your child until he has calmed himself down.

5. During the calm down period, your child does not exist. Don't make any eye contact. For a calm down period to end your child must calm down or gain control of himself for 2-3 seconds. Your child can call you names, strike your leg, or tantrum on the floor. But, until he calms down, he does not exist.

6. Don't underestimate the difficulty of ignoring your own child. Ignoring is work. At first, this will not be easy for you to do. The example of a vending machine for soft drinks may help to make this point. When a vending machine does not work properly, many adult's first reaction is to push, hit, and/or kick the machine. As you know, the coke machine does not respond, it ignores you. Soon, you walk away. Contrast this with slot machines. Slot machines may go periods without paying off, but then, unexpectedly, they pay off. For this reason, people will stand for hours putting money into a slot machine because they are infrequently rewarded for their efforts. You are encouraged to be a coke machine to your child when they are trying to self-calm. Stop paying attention to undesired behavior. Allow them the opportunity to calm themselves down without your assistance.
While you are ignoring, your child needs to be able to:

        See you.
        See you are not upset or frustrated.
        See what he is missing (the time-in).

7. What is he missing? Time-in! You can engage in an activity that you know he enjoys. Examples of such activities could be playing with their favorite toy or increasing time-in with a sibling. One mother perfected this one day when she slowly, bit by bit, ate the last piece of cheese until her son calmed down. After he calmed down, she shared the cheese. Remember, you are giving him the opportunity to learn self-control, a skill he will use throughout his life. It's far more humane to help a child develop self-quieting skills than it is to raise a child who "has a bad temper," or who has "trouble controlling his anger."

8. Big Picture. Even if it takes your child a month or two to learn how to calm himself down, having this skill can help to make your household a much more pleasant place to live.

Teaching Independent Play Skills—Infants

To encourage independent play activities:

1. Look for times when your infant is playing quietly by herself. Provide them with a lot of brief, nonverbal, physical contact.
2. Try to find an activity that you can engage in while you are also providing your infant with brief, physical contact. This might be reading the paper or a magazine or working on paper work that you brought home from the office.
3. Learn to discipline yourself to provide the physical contact during the time that you are engaged in a productive activity.
4. Gradually begin to go slightly longer and longer periods of time between touching your infant. The increases should be very small so that your infant never notices the increases are occurring.
5. Over time, perhaps two to four weeks, gradually decrease the frequency of your physical contact.

There are several points to consider:

- gradually wait longer and longer between physical touches
- in this way your infant will get the enjoyment out of playing alone and the affection from you from the same activity.

Teaching Independent Play Skills—Toddler

To encourage independent play activities:

1. Begin an activity with your toddler that you think they will enjoy. Play with them the whole time the first couple of times that you do it.

2. Provide many "love pats " during the play activity.

3. Pick an isolated play activity. An isolated play activity is an activity that is best performed by one person. For example, building Legos is something that children do well alone. A social play activity is an activity that requires two people in order to do it. An example would be playing catch with a ball.

4. Begin to excuse yourself from the activity at times when you can tell that your child is actively engaged. Excuse yourself for a very brief period of time, perhaps for only five seconds while you walk over to the kitchen counter and return directly to the activity. After about two days of excusing yourself for only 5 seconds, if your child can play for that 5 seconds, plan to be gone for 7 or 8 seconds. In this fashion gradually increase how long you are gone based upon your child continuing with his play while you are gone. What you are aiming for is to be able to leave without interrupting the activity that your toddler is doing.

5. Over time, perhaps two to three months, gradually stay away from your toddler for longer and longer periods of time, until you notice that you can be gone for extended periods of time. As you are able to excuse yourself for increasingly longer periods of time, don't forget to provide your toddler with periodic, brief, nonverbal, physical contact. In this way your

toddler will get the enjoyment out of playing and the affection from you from the same activity.

6. With time and practice, your toddler will learn how to entertain himself without the need for assistance from you. The more they play alone, the more they can accomplish on their own, and the more sense of satisfaction they will derive from their play activities.

Separation Anxiety

The first couple of times that you leave your child with a sitter or drop them off at a day-care center, it will probably be a very emotional experience for you. If you can treat these separations matter-of-factly, your child will learn to separate rather easily, making the whole process much less draining on both of you. Some additional suggestions follow.

1. Do not discuss the separation before it occurs. Doing so will not help, but it may make separation more difficult.

2. Plan ahead so that you can separate quickly. Have all of your child's things together in one bag or her toys out in one place so that you won't drag out the separation.

3. When it comes time to do so, separate as quickly and as matter-of-factly as possible.

4. If separating is hard for you, set up artificial opportunities to practice separating. For example, arrange to drop your child off at a friend or relative's house several additional times each week until you become more proficient at it.

5. When you pick your child up, don't be overly emotional. It's OK to act glad to see them, but don't start crying and hugging them excessively — to do so only shows them how hard the separation was for you.

6. Generally, the way children handle separation is a direct reflection of how their parents handle it. Do well and your child will do much better.

Effective Instruction-Giving

1. Be Directive.
Give instruction as a directive. Do not phrase instructions as questions. Questions do not relay behavioral expectations and give the child the option to say "no". "Please, pick up the book" is clearer than "Will you pick up the book?"

2. Near-at-hand.
Give instructions while standing within 3 feet of your child.

3. Quiet Voice.
Give instructions with a quiet toned or soft voice.

4. Make Eye Contact.
Have eye contact when giving an instruction. "John, look at me," may be the first instruction. Immediately provide praise. Then state, "John, put the yellow car in the toy box."

5. Be Clear.
Use clear and specific wording to tell the child what you want done. "Sue, place the blue marker in my hand."

6. Be Positive.
State the wanted behavior in a positive way. Decide what you want the child to be doing. Tell the child what you want him to "do" rather than what you "don't" want him to do. "John, walk." "Sue, put your fork in the sink." "Fred, put your coat on."

7. Wait.
After giving the instruction, wait 5 seconds. Do not repeat the instruction before giving the child a chance to respond.

8. Praise.
Praise the child immediately after he obeys.

Adapted from J. Olmi, Ph.D., USM School Psychology Service Center, Hattiesburg, MS. 1997
©Robert Ward and Matthew Hoag, 1977

Day Correction of Bedtime Problems

One of the most common concerns that parents of young children have is that they cannot get their children to bed at night or their children wake up in the middle of the night and cannot get back to sleep by themselves. The vast majority of the time these problems stem from the fact that your child does not have self-quieting skills. Self-quieting skills refer to a child's ability to quiet themselves when they begin to get upset about something. Most of the time, children with bedtime problems have had help or assistance from their parents in quieting at bedtime. This help may consist of nursing the child to sleep, or rocking the child to sleep, lying down with the child, or allowing the child to drift off to sleep in their parent's bed. The following strategies usually help a child to go to sleep alone:

1. Wake your child up at about the same time every morning. Be sure that you get them up while they are still playing quietly instead of waiting until they are crying.
2. Put your child to bed at about the same time every night. Put them to bed alone, awake, and tired.
3. Feed your child meals at about the same time every day.
4. Make sure that your child gets vigorous exercise every day.
5. Use *time-out* during the day for most misbehavior. Time-out should not be over until your child has self-quieted. Make sure that you are not avoiding any opportunities to use time-out. Every time-out helps with self-quieting skills.
6. Develop a routine for the last 30 minutes before bedtime that is quieting to your child and do not vary from it.

7. Use *time-in* during the day whenever your child is engaged in an activity that you consider acceptable.

8. Place several soft toys in your child's bed that can ultimately be used as "transition objects."

9. If you have to check him during the night, do not talk to the child, do not turn on the light, and do not pick the child up.

Once a child has developed self-quieting skills during the day, and they have had at least one week to practice these skills, they can usually learn to self-quiet at night within 3 to 4 nights.

Promoting Good Sleep Habits in Children

1. The child should be tired. This means that babies and toddlers need daily age-appropriate exercise. A young baby can get adequate exercise raising their head up and holding it up for short periods of time throughout the day. A slightly older baby can get adequate exercise bouncing in a walker or crawling around the house. A toddler can get exercise by going for long walks with one or both parents.

2. The child needs to be in a subdued environment. Holding a baby in a well lit family room while watching TV is hardly conducive to going to sleep. Placement in a crib in a dark room is one way to make it easier for a baby to go to sleep. For this reason, we usually discourage the use of nightlights in a baby's room and we suggest that the door to the baby's room be closed at bedtime. If the lights are off and the door closed from the newborn period on, the child will probably become accustomed to it and the parents probably won't have any problems with it.

3. The child needs to be relaxed. This relaxation will come about naturally if the parent will routinely place the baby in the crib and leave him alone until he has awakened from his sleep.

A practice that almost guarantees sleep problems, if continued for very long, is the practice of nursing or bottle feeding a baby to sleep. If a baby is nursed to sleep for the morning nap, the afternoon nap and for the night, the baby is learning nothing about going to sleep by himself and he is unlikely to develop any aids or transitional behaviors that he can use to help him to get to sleep by himself. Usually parents engage in these practices for their own enjoyment or comfort with little thought to what it is doing to the baby. They will report that their baby goes to sleep easily this way, with no concern for how the practice can be continued into the school age years.

The baby who separates well from his mother, goes to bed and gets up at consistent times, and gets an adequate amount of exercise during the day is much more likely to be able to get to sleep and stay asleep. Most parents who are awakened several times during the night don't feel their best the next day. The same thing is true for children. Once sleep problems are effectively dealt with, the children usually will feel and act better during the day.

Time-In

By their very dependent nature, newborns and young infants require a lot of physical contact from their parents. As they get older and their demand characteristics change, parents usually touch their children much less. By the time children are four years old, they are usually toilet trained, can get dressed and undressed themselves, can feed themselves, and can bathe themselves. Thus, if parents don't conscientiously put forth an effort to maintain a great deal of physical contact with their child, he or she will be touched much less than they were at earlier ages. There are several things that parents can do to help offset these natural changes.

1. Physical proximity. During the boring or distracting activities, place your child close to you where it is easy to reach him. At dinner, in the car, in a restaurant, when you have company, or when you are in a shopping mall, keep your child near you so that physical contact requires little, if any, additional effort on your part.

2. Physical contact. Frequent and brief (one or two seconds) nonverbal physical contact will do more to teach your child that you love him than anything else that you can do. Discipline yourself to touch your child at least fifty times each day for one or two seconds—touch him anytime that he is not doing something wrong or something that you disapprove of.

3. Verbal reprimands. Children don't have the verbal skills that adults do. Adults often send messages that are misunderstood by children, who may interpret verbal reprimands, nagging, and pleading as signs that their parents do not like them. Always keep in mind the old expression, "If you don't have anything nice to say, don't say anything at all. "

4. Nonverbal contact. Try to make most of your physical contact with children nonverbal. With young children, physical contact usually has a calming effect, whereas verbal praise, questioning, or general comments may only interrupt what your child was doing.

5. Independent play. Children need to have time to themselves—time when they can play, put things into their mouths, or stare into space. Generally, children don't do nearly as well when their parents carry them around much of the time and constantly try to entertain them. Keep in mind that, although your baby may fuss when frustrated, he or she will never learn to deal with frustration if you are always there to help them out. Give children enough freedom to explore the environment on their own, and they will learn skills that they can use the rest of their lives.

Remember:

Children need lots of brief, nonverbal physical contact. If you don't have anything nice to say, don't say anything at all.

Discipline for Toddlers

Time-out for toddlers involves placing your child in his playpen for a short period of time following each occurrence of a negative behavior. This procedure has been effective in reducing problem behaviors such as tantrums, hitting and other aggressive acts, failure to follow directions, and biting. Parents have found this method works much better than spanking, yelling, and threatening children. It is most appropriate for children ages nine months through two years.

A. **Preparations:**
　　1. A place for time-out should be selected, such as your child's playpen. It needs to be a dull place, but, *not* a dark, scary, or dangerous one. The aim is to remove the child to a place where not much is happening, *not* to make the child afraid.
　　2. Discuss with your spouse which behaviors will result in time-out.

B. **Procedures:**
　　1. Following the negative behavior, say to the child "Time-out for hitting." Say this calmly; no screaming, talking angrily, or nagging. Carry the child to the playpen, facing away from you and without talking to them.
　　2. When the child is in the playpen, wait until they have stopped crying for about two to five seconds. Before your child has stopped crying, do *not* look at, talk to, or talk about them. After they are finally quiet, just go over to the playpen, pick them up without sayting a word, and set them on the floor near some of their toys. Do not reprimand them or mention what they did wrong. Do not carry them around and console them.

3. After each time-out episode, toddlers should start out with a "clean slate." No discussion, nagging, threatening, or reminding is necessary. At the first opportunity, look for and praise positive behaviors. Catch 'em being good!

C. Summary of the rules:

    a. Decide about behaviors you will use time-out for ahead of time.

    b. Don't leave your child in time-out and forget about them.

    c. Don't nag, scold, or talk to your child when they are in time-out (all family members should follow this rule).

    d. Remain calm, particularly when your child is being testy.

    e. Don't use time-out for every problem.

From *Beyond Discipline: Parenting That Lasts a Lifetime* by Edward R. Christophersen. Published by Westport Publishers, Inc., Kansas City, MO.

Using Time-Out for Behavior Problems

A. Preparations:

1. Purchase a small portable kitchen timer.
2. Select a place for time-out. This could be a chair in the hallway, kitchen, or corner of a room. It needs to be a dull place (not your child's bedroom) where your child cannot view the TV or play with toys. It should not be a dark, scary, or dangerous place—the aim is to remove your child to a place where not much is happening, not to make him feel afraid.
3. Discuss with your spouse which behaviors will result in time-out. Consistency is very important.

B. Practicing (if your child is three or older):

1. Before using time-out for discipline, you should practice using it with your child at a pleasant time.
2. Tell your child there are two rules when in time-out:
   a. The timer will start only after he is quiet.
   b. Ask your child what will happen if he or she talks or makes noises when in time-out. Your child should say the timer will be reset.
3. After explaining the rules and checking out your child's understanding of the rules, go through the steps under "C" below. Tell your child you are "pretending " this time.
4. Mention to your child you will be using this technique instead of spanking, yelling, or threatening.

C. Procedures:

1. Following an inappropriate behavior, describe what your child did in as few words as possible. For example, say, "Time-out for hitting. " Say this calmly and only once.

Do not lose your temper or begin nagging. If your child has problems getting to the chair quickly, guide them with as little effort as needed. This can range from leading them part way by the hand to carrying them all the way to the chair. If you have to carry him, hold them facing away from you.

2. Practice with two-second time-outs initially, until you are certain the child understands they must be quiet in order to get up. Gradually increase the length of time they must sit. After you are using time-outs that are at least a minute long, begin to use the timer to signal the end of time-out.

3. The rule of thumb is a maximum of one minute of quiet time-out for each year of age. A two-year-old would have two minutes; a three-year-old, three minutes; and a five year-old, five minutes. For children five years and above, five minutes remain the maximum amount of time. If your child makes noises, screams, or cries, reset the timer. Do this *each* time the child makes any annoying noises. If your child gets off the chair before the time is up, replace them on the chair, and reset the timer. Do this each time the child gets off the chair.

4. After your child has been quiet and seated for the required amount of time, the timer will ring. Walk over to him, place your hand on his back and simply say, "Okay." Apply gentle pressure to their back with your hand for a second to let them know it's all right to get up now. Do not even comment on the time-out.

5. After a time-out period, your child should start with a "clean slate." Do not discuss, remind, or nag about what the child did wrong. Within five minutes after time-out, look for and praise good behavior. It's wise to take your child to a different part of the house and start them in a new activity.

Things to check when time-out doesn't work:

1. Be sure you are not warning your child one (or more) times before sending them to the time-out chair. Warnings only teach your child that they can misbehave at least once (or more) before you'll use time-out. Warnings make children's behavior worse, not better.

2. All adults who are responsible for disciplining your child at home should be using the time-out chair. You should agree when and for what behaviors to send your child to time-out. (You will want new sitters, visiting friends, and relatives to read and discuss the time-out guidelines.)

3. To maximize the effectiveness of time-out, you must make the rest of the day ("time-in") pleasant for your child. Remember to let your child know when they are well behaved rather than taking good behavior for granted. Most children would prefer to have you put them in time-out than ignore them completely.

4. Your child may say "Going to the chair doesn't bother me," or "I like time-out." Don't fall for this trick. Many children try to convince their parents that time-out is fun and therefore not working. You should notice over time that the problem behaviors for which you use time-out occur less often.

5. When you first begin using time-out, your child may act like time-out is a "game. " They may put themselves in time-out or ask to go there. If this happens, give your child what they want—that is, put them in time-out and require them to sit quietly for the required amount of time. They will soon learn that time-out is not a game. Your child may also laugh or giggle when being placed in time-out or while in time-out. Although this may aggravate you, it is important for you to ignore them completely when they are in time-out.

7. TV, radio, or a nice view out the window can make time-out more tolerable and prolong the length of time your child must stay in the chair by encouraging them to talk. Try to minimize such distractions.

8. You must use time-out for major as well as minor behavior problems. Parents have a tendency to feel that time-out is not enough of a punishment for big things. Consistency is most important for time-out to work for big and small problems.

9. Be certain that your child is aware of the rules that, if broken, result in time-out. Frequently, parents will establish a new rule ("Don't touch the new stereo ") without telling their children. When children unwittingly break the new rule they don't understand why they are being put in time-out.

10. Review the time-out guidelines to make certain you are following the recommendations.

When your child is in time-out:

a. Don't look at him or her.
b. Don't talk to him or her.
c. Don't talk about him or her.
d. Don't act angry.
e. Do remain calm.
f. Do follow the written guidelines.
g Do find something to do (read magazine, phone someone) when your child is crying and talking in time-out.
h. They should be able to see you.
i. They should be able to tell you're not mad.
j. They should be able to see what they are missing.

Redirecting Your Child's Activities

After your child has learned how to self-quiet, they need to learn how to redirect. Waiting until after they know how to self-quiet is critical because, if they cannot self-quiet, they will never be able to redirect. Thus, if you work on teaching them redirecting skills, before they have self-quieting skills, chances are you are only doing it to protect yourself from the unpleasant feelings that you get when they can't self-quiet or redirect.

1. When you see your child playing with one toy, or engaging in one activity for a period of time, and you sense that they may be just about finished with that activity or that they may be getting frustrated with it, then it's a perfect time to work on teaching them how to redirect their energies.
2. Begin by gradually joining their activity, either by playing with them or by talking to them while they are playing.
3. Try substituting another toy or activity that you know, from prior experience, that they might easily become interested in. In this way, they will begin to learn how to redirect from one activity to another.

It is critical that you put off teaching your child how to redirect until they have well-established, self-quieting skills.

Communicating with your Child

The word *communication* actually means listening. Most parents talk too much and listen too little.

With Your Baby

The earliest way to teach yourself how to communicate with your child is to begin communicating with them before they have any intelligible speech. Try repeating what your baby says as closely as you can. This may sound like gibberish to you but it may make good sense to your baby.

With Your Toddler

There are two cardinal rules with speech development in toddlers: be responsive to your child's speech and do not correct their speech. To be responsive all you have to do is engage in an activity when your child speaks to you. So, if they look at a glass of milk and say "Coke, " please do not correct them. Either pick up the glass, say "Coke, " or both pick up the glass and say "Coke. " In this way, your toddler will learn that speech serves an important function. Not correcting your child's speech may be difficult to do mainly because most of us are used to adults who can and do profit from being corrected. However, with a young child, they may take your correction as a sign that they did something wrong. It won't do any good to explain to them that you aren't mad at them. Just refrain from correcting them if you possibly can.

With Your School-aged Child

Identify one or two times and/or places where you will always listen to you child—where you will let your child talk about whatever she wants to talk about. The two most common places to listen to your child are rides in the car and when they are taking a bath. If you consistently speak only when spoken to, your child will come to appreciate these times. When you do respond to your child, try to be as nonjudgmental as possible. Just try to convey to your child that you understand what they are saying—it doesn't matter whether or not you agree with them, just that you listen to them and let them know that you understand what they are talking about.

About The Author

Dr. Christophersen is a clinical psychologist at The Children's Mercy Hospital in Kansas City, Missouri, where he is the Chief Psychologist for the APA-Approved Clinical Child Psychology Training Program. He is a Professor of Pediatrics at both the University of Missouri - Kansas City School of Medicine and the University of Kansas Medical Center.

For almost 30 years, Dr. Christophersen has lectured on child rearing to prenatal classes and seminars on parenting. He is a popular lecturer throughout the United States and Canada, addressing both professional meetings and meetings for the general public. He has appeared often on local and network television and radio programs and newspaper articles. He has made a total of over 800 personal appearances.

Dr. Christophersen has conducted extensive research on childrearing practices, having received approximately 6 million dollars in grants at the local, state, and federal level. He is a Fellow of the American Psychological Association (Clinical Psychology Division), the Society for Behavioral Medicine, and the Academy of Behavioral Medicine Research. He is also a Diplomate in Clinical Psychology of the American Board of Professional Psychology. He is in the National Registry of Health Service Providers in Psychology and is a Certified Psychologist in Kansas and Missouri. He has edited three issues of Pediatric Clinics of North America. He is the author of two other books for parents, Baby Owner's manual: What to Expect and How to Survive the First Year and Little People: Guidelines for Commonsense Child Rearing.

Dr. Christophersen received a Ph.D. in Developmental and Child Psychology from the University of Kansas in 1970. He lives with his wife and two children in suburban Kansas City.

The Third Edition
Baby Owner's Manual
Thoroughly Updated and Revised

The arrival of a baby comes with a great deal of excitement, wonder, curiosity, and activity. The nursery may be full of soft, pastel colors, stuffed animals and diapers, but the one thing babies don't bring with them to their new world is an owner's manual.

Dr. Christophersen gives the new baby owner a great deal of comfort and support in dealing with the baby's first year of life. His advice and information is very helpful and often humorous. Dr. Christophersen takes a practical view of babies; they all have fundamental needs of daily maintenance and efficient operation.

Baby Owner's Manual has been extensively revised and updated for this third edition. The importance of touching, participation by the father, and the development of self-quieting skills are new to this edition. For proud parents of a new arrival or those still expecting, no one should operate their new bundle of joy without *Baby Owner's Manual*.

* * *

In this book, Dr. Christophersen discusses:
Early Bonding
Safety in Nursery and Bath
Cleaning, Bathing, and Grooming
Sleeping Patterns and Fussiness
Feeding
Travel
and many more topics the first-time
parents will want to understand

* * *

Baby Owner's Manual is recommended by pediatricians, obstetricians, psychologists, teachers, and most of all-by parents.

ISBN 0-933701-31-4 $7.95

The Fourth Edition

Little People

Rearing Children is both the most delightful and the most trying experience most of us will ever be privileged to enjoy. It produces an overwhelming exhilaration that is difficult to explain, but impossible to get any other way. All parents have some problems with their children, yet almost every parent who has problems with a child is doing the best possible job of child rearing that he or she know how to do. Quite simply, child rearing is something that few parents are prepared or trained for. This book is for them—parents who for the most part are doing a good job, but who want to do better.

Dr. Christophersen takes the commonsense approach that children are little people, but still people. How well children are prepared for life and how much they will enjoy life has a lot to do with how they are raised.

Catch 'Em Being Good is one of Dr. Christophersen's favorite pieces of advice. The entire book, *Little People*, is built around guidelines that will help you encourage your child's emotional development and self-esteem. Dr. Christophersen's advice also comforts parents by discussing what is normal and acceptable behavior.

Little People is a positive book meant to help parents get the most out of the years they spend with the little people they bring into the world and help them grow up happy and healthy.

* * *

"Dr. Christophersen brings a fresh look...writes with humor and empathy."
Sun Newspapers

"Christophersen is refreshing...clear language."
Arizona Daily Star

"One of the most helpful resources..."
Salina Journal Sunflower

* * *

Little People is recommended by pediatricians, obstetricians, psychologists, teachers, and most of all—by parents.

ISBN 0-930851-05-6 $12.95

THE THINK SPACE™

The new low-stress way to manage
the challenging behaviors of young children

Tired of Time-Outs that don't work? Annoyed when your gentle warnings, countdowns and even threats are ignored? Time for a new look at discipline, and a visit to *The Think Space*. Early childhood specialists, Carolyn and Calvin Richert, have developed a new low-stress approach to child management that works with great consistency. In their book, the Richerts explain both the mindset and the technique that help children take responsibility for their own behavior while learning to honor the limits set by the adults in their lives.

Working with the advanced concepts of positive discipline, EQ (emotional intelligence) and the Montessori Method, the Richerts have developed a thoroughly positive approach that helps the child to focus on what TO DO "next time" instead of what he or she DID. Essentially, the Think Space is a sensitive way to give children time and space to process their conflicts without unnecessary confrontation with the adults in their lives.

Both parents and professionals (educators and childcare providers) are embracing this approach as one of the most effective tools yet developed for the safe and responsible management of those childhood behaviors that are intended to put adults on the defensive — angry crying, fussing, stubbornness, disruptiveness, tantrums, pouting, whining, negative attitudes.

With this approach you will learn how to establish calm and loving, yet firm leadership while nurturing the development of both responsibility and creativity in your child.

* * *

"Highly practical . . .works surprisingly well with preschoolers."
Parent/Provider Magazine

"Once learned, a child should be able to use this technique the rest of his life."
Dr. Edward R. Christophersen

"A quiet but effective structure . . . what happens is nothing short of miraculous."
Dr. Jerry A. Wyckoff

Calvin and Carolyn Richert both have Masters degrees in Education and over 27 years' experience in education and professional child care. For more than 15 of those years, they have been directors of their own childcare facility. In developing **The Think Space**, Calvin and Carolyn have had the unique advantage of working with many of the same children for up to four years in the natural setting of everyday life.

ISBN 0-9651971-9-0 $14.95

ORDER DIRECT: 1-888-22THINK (84465)

YES, I want _____ copies of Beyond Discipline for $10.95
YES, I want _____ copies of Little People for $12.95
YES, I want _____ copies of Baby Owner's Manual for $7.95
YES, I want _____ copies of The Think Space for $14.95

Please include shipping and handling of $2.50 Book Rate
OR **$3.50** UPS for 1st book; $.50 for each additional book

Method of Payment:

Check for $_____ to: Ship to: _____

Take V Publications   _____
P.O. Box 4490   _____
7200 West 83rd Street   _____
Shawnee Mission, KS 66204
Charge my credit card
☐ Visa   ☐ Master Charge   ☐ American Express   ☐ Discover
Account # _____   Exp. Date _____
Signature: _____
Phone # : _____

ORDER DIRECT: 1-888-22THINK (84465)

YES, I want _____ copies of Beyond Discipline for $10.95
YES, I want _____ copies of Little People for $12.95
YES, I want _____ copies of Baby Owner's Manual for $7.95
YES, I want _____ copies of The Think Space for $14.95

Please include shipping and handling of $2.50 Book Rate
OR $3.50 UPS for 1st book; $.50 for each additional book

Method of Payment:

Check for $_____ to: Ship to: _____

Take V Publications   _____
P.O. Box 4490   _____
7200 West 83rd Street   _____
Shawnee Mission, KS 66204
Charge my credit card
☐ Visa   ☐ Master Charge   ☐ American Express   ☐ Discover
Account # _____   Exp. Date _____
Signature: _____
Phone # : _____

Take V Publications
P.O. Box 4490
7200 West 83rd Street
Shawnee Mission, KS 66204

Take V Publications
P.O. Box 4490
7200 West 83rd Street
Shawnee Mission, KS 66204